Historical American Biographies

HENRY CLAY

From "War Hawk" to the "Great Compromiser"

Alison Davis Tibbitts

Enslow Publishers, Inc.

40 Industrial Road   PO Box 38
Box 398   Aldershot
Berkeley Heights, NJ 07922   Hants GU12 6BP
USA   UK

http://www.enslow.com

For my sons, Casey and Greg, and my husband,
Jonathan, who are the descendants of eight generations
of American military officers.

Copyright © 2003 Alison Davis Tibbitts

Library of Congress Cataloging-in-Publication Data

Tibbitts, Alison.
    Henry Clay : from "war hawk" to the "Great Compromiser" / Alison
Davis Tibbitts.
       p. cm. — (Historical American biographies)
    Summary: A biography of the American statesman best remembered
for his initiation and support of political compromise to keep the Union
together during the first half of the nineteenth century.
    Includes bibliographical references and index.
    ISBN 0-7660-1980-2
    1. Clay, Henry, 1777-1852—Juvenile literature. 2. Legislators—United
States—Biography—Juvenile literature. 3. United States. Congress.
Senate—Biography—Juvenile literature. 4. United States—Politics and
government—1815-1861—Juvenile literature. [1. Clay, Henry,
1777–1852. 2. Statesmen. 3. Legislators. 4. United States—Politics and
government—1815-1861.] I. Title. II. Series.
E340.C6T53 2003
973.5'092—dc21

                            2002156458

Printed in the United States of America

10 9 8 7 6 5 4 3 2 1

To Our Readers:
We have done our best to make sure all Internet Addresses in this book were
active and appropriate when we went to press. However, the author and the pub-
lisher have no control over and assume no liability for the material available on
those Internet sites or on other Web sites they may link to. Any comments or sug-
gestions can be sent by e-mail to comments@enslow.com or to the address on the
back cover.

Illustration Credits: Architect of the Capitol, p. 114; Casey Tibbitts, p.
16; Courtesy of Ashland, the Henry Clay Estate in Lexington, Kentucky,
pp. 8, 21, 45, 69, 74, 83; Enslow Publishers, Inc., pp. 64, 97, 110;
National Archives and Records Administration, pp. 32, 98, 103;
Reproduced from the *Dictionary of American Portraits*, published by
Dover Publications, Inc., in 1967, pp. 86, 102; U.S. Senate Collection,
pp. 4, 12, 54;

Cover Illustration: U.S. Senate Collection (Clay Portrait and
Background)

CONTENTS

Henry Clay

1

HENRY CLAY'S BURDEN

The tall, slender man in his early seventies climbed into a carriage and settled himself by the window. He wore his usual black suit and white shirt with a high collar that brushed against his hair. After greeting his fellow travelers, he lapsed into deep, silent thought. This man, Henry Clay, did not seem to take notice of the bright autumn leaves as they drifted downward in the crisp air of early November 1849.

A Country in Turmoil

Senator Henry Clay's thoughts may have been focused on the fact that the United States was in serious trouble. Former President John Tyler had signed a resolution to admit Texas, formerly part of Mexico, into the Union. Texas officially became a state on December 29, 1845. However, Mexico had not completely given up its claim to Texas. The country could not agree with the United States on a boundary for the state. The two nations went to war, and the United States was victorious. Under the Treaty of Guadalupe Hidalgo, signed in 1848, the United States gained land covering all of present-day California, Nevada, and Utah, and parts of present-day Arizona, New Mexico, Colorado, and Wyoming. Settlers began moving to the new region.

Westward migration in the late 1840s was causing major problems for Congress. The most troublesome were centered around the institution of slavery, pitting slave states against Free States. People in the North and South did not understand each other very well, especially where slavery was concerned. Border states had many residents on both sides of the issue.

The South's economy depended almost entirely on farming. The region needed thousands of field hands to plant and harvest crops to be sold in American and European markets. Most of the workers were slaves descended from Africans brought to America decades earlier.

Meanwhile, the North's thriving economy was based on machinery. Far fewer workers were needed to make an ever-growing selection of products. The North did not permit slavery and some northerners believed it should be abolished throughout the country. These northerners were called abolitionists.

The U.S. Senate worked to maintain its delicate balance between the slave states and Free States. Each state had two senators regardless of the size of its population, and each vote carried equal weight. This balance was particularly important when slavery issues were involved.

Membership in the House of Representatives was determined by the size of each state's population. States with more people had more representatives and, therefore, greater political power in the House than did those states with fewer citizens.

Many northerners felt that the South had an unfair advantage when it came to counting a state's population. Slaves had no representation in Congress and they could not vote. They were not always counted accurately in the populations of Southern states. The U.S. Constitution's "three-fifths rule" allowed Southerners to include three-fifths, or 60 percent, of their slaves in a census. Northerners worried that someday Texas could be divided into four or five separate states that allowed slavery. This would give the South the majority of states and increased political strength.

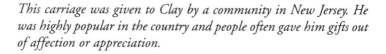

Clay and His Country

Henry Clay was on a vital mission to the nation's capital in Washington. He knew well the heavy burden he carried. He had been handed the fate of the nation and asked to fix it.

Clay had spent nearly forty years in the United States Congress trying to solve the country's most serious problems. During that time, he had dealt with tough rivals and guided America successfully through financial crises, wars, social upheavals, new

This carriage was given to Clay by a community in New Jersey. He was highly popular in the country and people often gave him gifts out of affection or appreciation.

territories, boundary disputes, American Indian issues, and slavery issues.

A grave challenge awaited his return to a Congress facing crucial issues. Clay had to answer such questions as: How, or perhaps why, should the California, New Mexico, and the Utah territories be brought into the Union? How would Congress resolve the boundary dispute between Texas and New Mexico? Could any or all of this be done without civil war? Every question led to several others.

One question involved the Wilmot Proviso. This clause, sponsored by Congressman David Wilmot of Pennsylvania, was attached to a funding bill going through the House of Representatives in mid-summer 1846. The proviso stated that slavery must never be allowed on any lands that the United States would acquire from Mexico in the future. Many saw Wilmot's plan as part of the overall effort to prevent further expansion of slavery.

The House had passed the proviso on August 8, 1846. However, it failed in the Senate two days later. It appeared in other bills for a few years without passage and, in 1849, was still unresolved.

Clay encountered many agreements and disagreements in his career. His best assets for dealing with them were a razor-sharp mind and an ability to persuade others to his points of view. Clay's quick temper and harsh wit sometimes worked against him. However, he never lost his passion about what he thought was best for the nation.

His journey would keep him away from Ashland, his home in Lexington, Kentucky, for a long time. He and his wife, Lucretia, had celebrated their fiftieth wedding anniversary a few months earlier, on April 11, 1849. He still depended heavily on her. Lucretia was a capable, careful money manager, which Clay appreciated. During their fifty years of marriage, she suffered many fears and heartaches alone while her husband was away from home. However, Lucretia rarely complained.

Arrival in Washington

Clay came out of his preoccupation as the carriage slowed to a stop. He collected his books and traveling case and set out to join some friends. After short visits in Philadelphia and New York, he boarded the train for Washington. It stopped overnight in Baltimore, Maryland, where a cheering crowd welcomed him.

Another sizable gathering followed Clay all the way to his hotel. He was exhausted from the journey, and he asked to meet with them the following morning.

Early the next day, Clay shook many outstretched hands. He discussed the dangers facing the nation and promised to work toward reducing the terrible prospect of civil war. In addition, he noted that the regions acquired from the Mexican War had too little water to support large crops, especially those requiring slaves. He added that he doubted slavery could succeed in California or New Mexico because the citizens would never allow it.

When he arrived in Washington on December 1, Clay left his calling card at the White House to inform President Zachary Taylor of his arrival. He went to the National Hotel and settled into his usual Suite 32 on the second floor. It had a comfortable bedroom and sitting room for thirty dollars a week. James Marshall, Clay's longtime valet and a free African American, oversaw all needs for his comfort.[1]

Clay drew crowds everywhere he went. They were often so large that he could not talk very long to more than a few people. He met with members of Congress and the Cabinet. He dined with President Taylor at the White House on December 13, 1849, two weeks after his arrival.

Cheers and applause greeted Clay's return to Congress. Senators John C. Calhoun of South Carolina and Daniel Webster of Massachusetts led members in expressing their worries about keeping the Union together. They felt time was running out.

Congressmen, young and old from North and South, knew about Clay's ability to find solutions, even in the worst situations. He had proven several

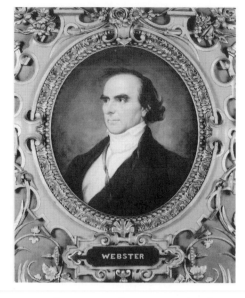

Artist Adrian Lamb painted this oil on canvas portrait of Daniel Webster of Massachusetts. Webster was one of the many statesmen that worked with Henry Clay.

times that he could craft a compromise acceptable to people of various parties and viewpoints. Even if his plans were imperfect, they usually were the best ones at the time.

Clay sometimes worked to the point of exhaustion and illness. He persuaded, threatened, and begged Congress to take the actions that were necessary to preserve the Union. He was widely known as "The Great Compromiser." He could not foretell the outcome of the grave threat to the nation. For Henry Clay, there was only one goal: one indivisible Union.

2

THE EARLY YEARS

Henry Clay was born on April 12, 1777, during the Revolutionary War. Reverend John and Elizabeth Hudson Clay welcomed their seventh child just nine months after a document called the Declaration of Independence severed America's ties with Great Britain.

Some of Reverend Clay's ancestors had come to the New World from England 170 years earlier. Henry's great-great-great grandfather, Captain John Clay, arrived in 1613 when Jamestown was an unstable six-year-old colony in Virginia. Early settlers encountered cold winters, hot and humid summers, failed crops, wild animals, and American Indians who sometimes threatened their lives. Many families ventured inland searching for safer places to live.

A Reverend's Son

Shortly before Henry was born, the family moved to a 464-acre farm in Virginia owned by Elizabeth Clay's father, George Hudson.[1] The comfortable two-story home was in the low, swampy, slave-holding region of Hanover County known as the Slashes. The name came from tall thickets of grasses and reeds that grew there.

Reverend Clay freely practiced his energetic style of Baptist religion without interference. Friends nicknamed him "Sir John" after his ancestor, Sir John Clay of Wales, the father of Captain John Clay of Jamestown.

Frontier Life

The early years of the war with Great Britain were hard for all settlers. Life was especially hard for those that lived far from large populations. British soldiers still stirred fear and violence across the countryside, as they had for years. A favorite hostile act of the British was to supply weapons to American Indians and encourage them to stage sneak attacks on settlers.

Settlers along the frontier were responsible for their own safety. If and when they needed more protection, they sought help from hunters and explorers such as Daniel Boone and George Rogers Clark. Boone, Clark, and other frontiersmen worked with groups of volunteers who knew the lay of the land. They tried to stop raiding parties before settlers could be hurt. One night in 1778, Clark and a small band successfully stormed three enemy outposts, one after another. The British soldiers and their American Indian friends attacked far less often after that.

Two tragic events occurred when Henry was four years old. Reverend Clay died in 1781, leaving his wife to care for five sons and three daughters. Henry was too young to have lasting memories of his father.

Not long after Reverend Clay's death, the brutal British Lieutenant Colonel, Banastre Tarleton, led a raiding party through the Slashes. His troops attacked the Clays' farm along with many others. They looted the house and destroyed everything they could not carry away. Young Henry watched the soldiers hunt for buried treasure. They plunged their swords deep into the fresh graves of Reverend Clay and Henry's grandfather, George Hudson.

Henry began attending the Old Field School in the Slashes when he was seven. Master Peter Deacon taught basic reading, writing, and arithmetic in a small building with a dirt floor, one door, and no

Henry Clay spent his youth in a wooded area of Virginia known as the Slashes. British soldiers roamed and raided the homes and farms in the region during the Revolutionary War.

windows. Henry also spent several years studying in St. Paul's Church.

He enjoyed learning about the writings of Virginia's leaders. Many important men traveled across the state making public speeches and meeting the people. Virginia's first governor, Patrick Henry, lived in Hanover County and he often spoke in public.

A New Family

Elizabeth Clay was thirty-two when she remarried in 1782. Her second husband, Henry Watkins, was a twenty-six-year-old planter and militia captain. He also was the brother-in-law of one of her sisters. The couple moved her family sixteen miles to his home in the town of Richmond. They eventually had seven babies of their own, giving the combined family a total of fifteen children.

Watkins had good relationships with the Clay children. He took a special interest in Henry's bright mind and willingness to work. He helped Henry find a job as an errand boy at a store owned by Richard Denny. Henry spent most of his free time reading on many subjects.

The Watkins family decided in 1791 to move to Kentucky in the West, where the captain's brother, John, had a successful business. The Watkins family wanted Henry, then fourteen, to stay in Richmond and study for a career in the law.

Gaining Experience

Watkins asked for help from his friend, Colonel Thomas Tinsley. The colonel's brother, Peter Tinsley, was clerk of the Virginia High Court of Chancery in Richmond.[2] After some time and a little pressure from Watkins, the Chancery hired Henry. Henry settled in quickly and the staff accepted him with enthusiasm. His cheerful, outgoing personality and close attention to details made him a welcome addition.

While at the Chancery, Henry worked hard to perfect distinctive and recognizable handwriting. A vital part of his job was to record every word exactly as lawyers read them to him. He wrote many copies of documents and letters for court records and distribution. Each was penned in his angular script almost exactly as the original.

Chancellor George Wythe watched Henry work for some time before asking about him. Wythe was nearing seventy and painful arthritis made it hard for him to write. He asked Peter Tinsley for an appraisal of Henry's work and received a glowing report. In 1792, when Henry was fifteen years old, the chancellor hired him as his private secretary.

This was a rare stroke of good luck. Wythe was a signer of the Declaration of Independence. He had been for many years a law professor at the College of William and Mary in Williamsburg, Virginia. Thomas Jefferson, James Madison, and John Marshall were among his students.

Henry was honored to work with someone of Wythe's stature. After Kentucky became the fifteenth state on June 1, 1792, Wythe and Henry had long talks about the state's future. They also discussed the books Henry had read at Denny's store.

Wythe offered books from his own library to broaden Henry's education. Henry studied the writings of the ancient Greeks and Romans. He enjoyed classical literature and histories of the world, even when he stumbled over some of the translations. Wythe urged him to explore new ideas and reexamine old ones.

Henry was so happy with his growing education that he decided to form a debate club. The members were good friends with whom he wanted to share his new knowledge.

The job at the Chancery provided some unexpected advantages. Wythe often invited Henry to dinners and parties where he met the educated, wealthy, well-connected social leaders of Richmond. These events polished his social skills, broadened his political views, and taught him to relax in any situation.

When Henry left the Chancery in 1796, he knew his career would be in the law. He accepted an offer to work with Attorney General Robert Brooke, a Revolutionary War hero. He would also lodge in Brooke's home.[3] Brooke helped Henry prepare for his bar examination. This is a difficult test every lawyer must pass before obtaining a license to practice law. Henry passed, and he received his law license in 1797.

The Young Lawyer

The new lawyer had to decide whether or not to stay in Virginia. He considered the tight competition for cases among the town's young lawyers. He believed Richmond was a safer, more secure place than the rough-and-tumble frontier where he had grown up. He decided to move to central Kentucky. He would be near his family and all the opportunities awaiting an honest, hardworking lawyer.

Clay left for the West in November 1797. Many other educated young men also were bringing fresh ideas to the region. He arrived in early December and found lodgings through his older brother. John Clay was a successful businessman in Lexington. The brothers' parents lived twelve miles away in the small town of Versailles.

Clay went to Fayette County's Court of Quarter Sessions on March 20, 1798. He presented his Virginia license and filed a request to practice law in Kentucky. He took the required oaths and received his license. He was ready.

Clay took time to become familiar with his surroundings. He worked for new friends recommended by George Wythe. Clay met many people and traveled the countryside, studying the area and organizing his legal practice.

Clay was known within a year as the man to see about lawsuits involving land disputes. He decided to become the local expert on the subject because land was very important to Kentucky's economy. This specialty within the law offered many career

This portrait shows Clay early in his career as a young lawyer and politician, before his many responsibilities and various bouts of ill health aged him before his time.

possibilities. Clients paid him in cash or in land of equal value.

Kentucky's muddle of land management procedures had no directions or uniform standards for guidance. Clay had to resolve disputes to the satisfaction of all parties involved. This was rarely easy.

Each land ownership case was different. Many involved old deeds that had been prepared before 1792, when Kentucky was still part of Virginia. Sometimes sales were invalid because they had not been entered into the county records. Clay often searched long and hard for missing documents. He often received paperwork with incorrect or incomplete information about buyers and sellers.

Some older properties had been traded without a written agreement, such as an exchange of land for animals or water rights. Land surveys and boundary lines were often unclear or inaccurate. Problems arose when two owners claimed the same land.

His practice was not limited to land matters. Clay also became a skilled criminal attorney who preferred to defend the accused rather than to prosecute the case. Frontier justice could be tough. Clay's deep voice, dramatic gestures, and powers of persuasion seldom were seen in the West. He used them to great advantage.

Clay was effective in the courtroom. He planned his legal cases with careful attention to detail. His arguments were so convincing that a noted historian and editor wrote, ". . . no person was ever hanged in a trial where Clay appeared for the defense."[4]

His reputation grew as he won more and more cases. He soon earned acceptance into the small circle of Kentucky's finest lawyers. Lexington's quick growth and expansion kept Clay's calendar full.

A Social Life

Despite his dedication to the law, Clay was not an all-work-and-no-play fellow. His years at the Chancery had taught him the importance of accepting invitations to parties, dinners, and other social events. He was the center of conversations on many subjects. His nimble mind and relaxed manner made him a popular and sought-after guest.

Clay loved to play poker and he excelled at bluffing, or exaggerating the strength of his hand. Poker had a lot in common with debates and courtroom arguments. All required understanding the art of give-and-take, knowing when to move ahead or to step back, and when to stop.

Clay joined Lexington's Rhetorical Society, an established and more serious version of the debate club he began in Richmond. He liked meeting the members and taking part in their lively talks about history, philosophy, economy, and especially politics.

3

BEGINNING A POLITICAL CAREER

The Federalist and Democratic-Republican parties competed to lead the country at the end of the eighteenth century. The Federalists favored a strong and powerful central government. The Democratic-Republicans believed government power belonged in the hands of the people.

Speaking Out

It did not take Clay long to develop an interest in politics. One afternoon in 1798, he and his friend, George Nicholas, attended a public rally near Lexington. They came to hear the noisy crowd's opinions on the despised Alien and Sedition Acts.

The Alien Act included a Naturalization Act with strict requirements that foreigners had to satisfy before applying for American citizenship. The Naturalization Act also raised the residence requirement from five to fourteen years before one could apply for citizenship.

The Sedition Act stated that anyone who wrote or published misleading, untrue, or disgraceful articles in papers about the president, Congress, or the government would be prosecuted.[1] The statement violated the Constitution's First Amendment right of free speech, and most of those arrested and convicted were Democratic-Republican editors.

George Nicholas was among the first speakers at the rally against these acts. He described ways that they violated the U.S. Constitution. He was sincere, but his words did not satisfy the emotional crowd. As Clay listened, some men nudged him toward the front of the crowd and lifted him onto a wagon, urging him to speak.

Seeing the frustration in people's faces, Clay seized the moment. He angrily spoke against the injustice and blackmail of the acts. He described their unlawful violations of personal rights, states' rights, and the U.S. Constitution. He sympathized with the fear and humiliation citizens and aliens felt at being threatened with stiff fines or prison terms for mistakes.

When he finished, the silent crowd burst into applause for the young speaker barely into his twenties. Men hoisted Clay and Nicholas onto their shoulders and carried them to a nearby carriage. People surrounded and cheered them as they rode through town.

Marriage

Henry Clay's life changed on April 11, 1799, the day before his twenty-second birthday. He married eighteen-year-old Lucretia Hart in her family home on Mill Street in Lexington. The couple settled into their own home on Mill Street near Clay's law office.

Born in Hagerstown, Maryland, on March 18, 1781, the bride was the daughter of Colonel Thomas and Suzanna Gray Hart. She had dark hair and brown eyes.

Lucretia had plenty of spirit and Clay enjoyed that. She was kind and showed promise of being a good homemaker and money manager. She also did not gossip. In the nineteenth century, these were valuable qualities for the wife of any man who planned to move in high circles and might be away from home for long periods.

Lucretia's father came from Hanover County, Virginia, and was a founder of the Transylvania Company. This important financial resource helped early settlers moving to Kentucky. The Harts had come to Lexington to oversee their vast land holdings when Lucretia was three. They soon became part of the town's inner circle. Such connections could be a powerful asset for anyone considering a political career.

Early Politics

Several merchants and businessmen thought Clay's legal skills would be valuable in state government. With his approval, they submitted his name during the summer of 1803. After little or no campaigning, Clay won his first election to the Kentucky Legislature the following November.

Kentucky's capital is in Frankfurt, near Lexington. The legislature met there part-time, so Clay was able to continue his law practice. He greatly admired President Thomas Jefferson, then in his first term. Jefferson's Republican ideals shaped Clay's views on many issues. Both men believed in states' rights, whereby each state made decisions without undue pressure from the federal government. Supporters of states' rights were opposed to Federalists, who concentrated political power in a strong central government.

The Clays' first child, Henrietta, was born in 1800 and died eleven days before her first birthday. Two healthy sons, Theodore Wythe and Thomas Hart, were born in 1802 and 1803. Lucretia delivered their fourth child, Susan Hart, in 1805.

As Clay's law work prospered, Lexington's Transylvania University appointed him a professor of law on October 10, 1805. He was a natural teacher who loved discussing the law with his students. They learned that dramatic flair, a strong vocabulary, and bits of humor helped to win cases.

The Senate

In the nineteenth century, Kentucky voters elected their legislators who, in turn, chose the state's members in the U.S. Senate. On November 19, 1806, the legislature voted 68 to 10 to send Clay to Washington to fill the last four months of Senator John Adair's term.[2] Adair resigned after he was not reelected. Clay left Transylvania University with an agreement that he would return someday.

Clay's valet, Aaron Dupuy, accompanied him to Washington. The city's gray skies did not impress them. Rain soaked the unpaved streets and carriages splashed mud as they passed. The men hurried to the warmth of Frost and Quinn's boardinghouse near the Capitol.

Clay took the oath of office on December 29, 1806. If people knew that Kentucky's junior senator was five months younger than the Constitutional requirement that a senator must be at least thirty years old, they said nothing. The session ended on March 3, 1807. Clay went home to his family, resumed his law practice, and pursued his community interests.

Clay had spent his Washington months well, meeting many people and observing the Senate at work. Because he could discuss almost any subject, he was comfortable with high government officials. He met Secretary of State James Madison, Treasury Secretary Albert Gallatin, and Senator John Quincy Adams of Massachusetts.

President Jefferson

Soon after his arrival, Clay paid a courtesy call on President Thomas Jefferson. The president considered the capital "a dreary scene where envy, hatred, malice, revenge, and all the worst passions of men . . . make one another as miserable as possible."[3] His opinion was formed in part from his bad experiences with Aaron Burr.

In the 1800 presidential race, Jefferson and Burr had received seventy-three electoral votes each. The tie went to the House for resolution. Burr would not compromise with the Federalists who controlled the House. After three dozen votes in six days, the House elected Jefferson on February 17.[4] Burr became vice-president. He and Jefferson clashed frequently throughout their term.

In 1804, Burr had a serious dispute with former Treasury Secretary Alexander Hamilton. They dueled in Weehawken, New Jersey, on July 11, and Burr killed Hamilton. When his vice-presidential term ended in early 1805, Burr went to New York. There, Republicans blocked his nomination for governor, but he ran anyway and lost.

Aaron Burr

To escape bad publicity after Hamilton's death, Burr went west. There, dueling was an accepted form of self-defense. He gave different versions of his plans, depending on the listener. He visited Andrew Jackson at home in Kentucky, where he purposely misled the general. Burr told a tale about needing boats and the names of reliable officers. He claimed they were needed to defend the United States against an expected Spanish attack. Jackson had no reason to doubt him, and he agreed to help.

Burr actually was plotting with Spain to seize the Louisiana Territory and declare it, and other nearby lands, an independent nation. Burr's co-conspirator, General James Wilkinson, commanded the American troops in New Orleans. Burr had convinced him that fame and fortune awaited if he joined the plot.

Joseph Hamilton Daveiss, U.S. district attorney in Frankfort, had been tracking Burr. He warned Jefferson repeatedly of rumors about Burr's activities,

Louisiana Territory

President Thomas Jefferson acquired the Louisiana Territory in 1803. The United States paid $15 million for 828,000 square miles of land from the Rocky Mountains up to and including the Mississippi River.[5] Jefferson was pleased with the amount of land Emperor Napoleon Bonaparte of France offered to sell when his plans for a French Empire in North America collapsed.[6] Jefferson sealed the bargain and the Senate approved the purchase by a vote of 26 to 5.

but received no reply. Daveiss proceeded on his own to request a grand jury. He wanted to determine whether Burr was planning an attack on Mexico and Florida to provoke war with Spain.[7] Senator John Adair, a key witness, was unavailable and the first case was dismissed.

Daveiss requested a second grand jury hearing. Burr asked Clay to be his lawyer. Clay hesitated because he had to leave for his new Senate seat in Washington. Refusing a fee, he agreed to stay if Burr would write a statement declaring his complete innocence of all charges. Burr did so. At the December hearing, Clay's faith in Burr led him to say he would ". . . instantly renounce Col. Burr and his cause, did he entertain the slightest idea of his guilt, as to the charges exhibited against him by Mr. Daveiss."[8]

Clay accused the court of severe prejudice against Burr. In the hearing, Senator Adair said he knew of no evidence to indict Burr.[9] The newspaper, *Western World*, also changed its position after weeks of anti-Burr articles. The staff claimed they had no firsthand knowledge of illegal activity. The case was dismissed again.

Clay left for Washington the next morning and had gone just a few miles when he heard shocking news. President Jefferson had warned the nation about a military plot to destroy the United States. He issued a proclamation concerning "serious

This is a very early daguerreotype of President's House in Washington, D.C. The city was undeveloped in the early 1800s. Buildings were not close together and roads were unpaved.

danger and stopping movement of Burr's men and equipment down the Mississippi."[10]

Henry Clay was stunned. As a lawyer, he had to see proof before he could believe the news. When he paid a courtesy call on Thomas Jefferson at the President's House, he was shown evidence from Wilkinson, who had submitted it in an effort to save himself.

Aaron Burr was put on trial for treason in U.S. Circuit Court. Burr's friend, Chief Justice John Marshall, presided over the case and acquitted him. Jefferson sent Clay a confidential letter through Attorney General Caesar A. Rodney. In it, he asked whether Clay would represent Burr if he was tried again in Ohio.

Clay declined with deep thanks for Jefferson's confidence in him. Clay wrote to his son, Thomas Hart, on December 1, 1807, that he would never give Burr "an opportunity of deceiving him a second time."[11]

The Supreme Court

Clay's law practice took a step forward about that time. He defended his first two cases before the U.S. Supreme Court in Washington. It was a valuable experience, but while he argued with passion and persuasion, he lost both cases.

James Madison became America's fourth president in 1808. Kentucky's legislature returned Clay to the U.S. Senate, where he took the oath of office on January 4, 1810. He replaced his friend, Buckner Thruston, who resigned fourteen months before his term ended.[12] Because Clay came from a border state, he could describe the many opportunities beyond the Mississippi River.

The House of Representatives

Clay's first election to the U.S. House of Representatives came in August 1810. Following the oath on March 4, 1811, members elected him Speaker on the first ballot during the first day of the session.

Clay knew the Speaker's role traditionally had had little or no influence over the course of House politics.[13] He intended to make major changes that would allow him to guide legislation and control decisions. According to modern-day Supreme Court justice Sandra Day O'Connor, his hard work was "largely responsible for increasing the responsibilities and power of the Speaker."[14] He chose chairmen who agreed with him and would support his political agenda. He put the speaker's influence to good use.[15]

War Hawks

The 1810 election changed the makeup of Congress. Half the older House members, who resisted war, were defeated. Their places went to energetic, passionate young men called the "War Hawks." They dominated Congress, where Speaker Clay and Congressman John C. Calhoun of South Carolina were the most outspoken new leaders.

The War Hawks, with other southern and western members, resented Britain's Orders in Council. The Orders in Council disregarded the neutral position of the United States at sea. American ships were subject to attack, search, or capture at any time. The orders also prevented the United States from trading with European countries controlled by Emperor Napoleon Bonaparte of France. The British did not want competition for their markets. The War Hawks demanded that the Orders in Council be withdrawn at once, but Britain refused. Southerners and Westerners favored war to push Great Britain out of America. New Englanders did not want war because they feared it would hurt their struggling shipping businesses.

The War Hawks had goals beyond America's rights as a neutral nation. Because they wanted more land, they urged the people of the Northwest Territory and Florida to become part of the United States. Though some Florida settlers rebelled against

Spain in 1812, their rebellion was unsuccessful. Meanwhile, American Indians, aided by the British, clashed with Northwesterners over land while Southerners wanted more markets for their products.

Clay began his second term in the House and was reelected speaker in March 1812. The War Hawks prodded Madison toward war because they deeply resented Britain's refusal to honor America's neutrality at sea. They felt this was a matter of national pride. However, Clay's opponents accused him of war-mongering.

President Madison asked Congress to take action on June 1, 1812. A declaration of war against Great Britain followed on June 18. The House voted 79 to 49, and the Senate voted 19 to 13 in favor of the declaration.

4

NEGOTIATIONS IN EUROPE

The Americans fared badly in the first year of the War of 1812. The U.S. Army had little success in its North American battles. The situation improved when the U.S.S. *Constitution* and other American naval vessels began holding their own against Britain's powerful Royal Navy. Captain Oliver Hazard Perry and his eight-vessel fleet scored a major victory on Lake Erie, smashing through a British blockade in three hours. Perry sent a message to President Madison, stating, "We have met the enemy and they are ours."[1]

After Perry's victory at Lake Erie, General William Henry Harrison led his forces into Canada.

He won the Battle of the Thames while the British lost their American Indian ally, Tecumseh.

Belgium

Clay won his third Congressional election and took office in March 1813. However, at Madison's request, he resigned from the House on January 19, 1814. The president had appointed him one of five American commissioners to a peace conference in Belgium.

Clay sailed from New York to Gottenburg, Sweden. On June 2, he began traveling by coach through Denmark, Holland, and Germany. He particularly enjoyed Holland's beautiful countryside and friendly people. He was most impressed by the "innumerable herds of the finest cows I had ever beheld."[2]

He arrived in the city of Ghent, Belgium, three weeks later, on June 28. British and American representatives there had spent the previous year arguing. They disagreed over everything until the conference began. Madison's general orders to the commissioners were to prepare a treaty to end the War of 1812, known to his Federalist opponents as Mr. Madison's War.

The Delegates

The American delegation lodged at Hotel des Pays Bas before moving to the more spacious Hotel Lovendeghem.[3] Clay's four colleagues included Minister to Russia John Quincy Adams and Minister to Sweden Jonathan Russell. Another was former Treasury Secretary Albert Gallatin, who resigned from Madison's Cabinet to attend the conference. His son, James, was his secretary.

Senator James Bayard of Delaware was the fourth member. He and Gallatin brought Madison's stepson, John Payne Todd, to serve as a general secretary. Bayard was a Federalist, a Princeton University graduate, lawyer, and world traveler of great charm and sophistication. During their earlier dealings in Russia, he had considered Adams stiffly formal, critical, and unyielding. The fifth man was Henry Clay, accompanied by his secretary, Henry Carroll, and his valet, Aaron Dupuy.

The American government sent high-level negotiators to Europe. Britain's lower ranking personnel lacked any authority. Their instructions were to send all documents to London for review and approval before agreeing to anything.

John Quincy Adams

Adams was the committee chairman and he prepared all communications to the British. His colleagues often disputed his methods of handling just about everything. The men had met before, and some were friends, but their differences became obvious during the six months they lived and worked in the same hotel.

Adams had not brought a secretary, so he had to make copies of all correspondence himself. He became crankier each day and preferred to have his meals alone. Clay finally persuaded him to dine with the others by implying that they thought he was rude. Adams would not allow himself to be improper, so he dined with the group after that.

John Quincy Adams actually was a shy, reserved man. He was unlike any of his colleagues, especially Henry Clay. He resented Clay's relaxed manner and dry sense of humor. He minded when Russell agreed with Clay's opinions and followed his lead. Adams disapproved when the others gathered after dinner to drink wine and smoke cigars. He took offense when Clay swore and talked fast when telling stories. He became upset when Clay drank whiskey, played cards, and gambled.

Adams wrote in his diary that Clay asked if he knew how to play poker. Adams replied that he had forgotten. Clay said the secret to beating an opponent was "holding your hand, with a solemn and confident phiz [face], and outbragging him."[4] Adams often wrote that Clay and his friends were going to bed at the same time that Adams was waking up.[5] Adams was known to wake up at dawn.

London's long silences exasperated the Americans. They began to squabble among themselves as weeks passed without a word. Finally, the British sent their one and only offer to settle the war. The British demanded that America meet the following terms:

1. Give control of the Great Lakes to Britain.
2. Grant free access to the entire Mississippi River.
3. Create a route from Nova Scotia to Quebec by crossing Maine.
4. Allow an independent state for Britain's American Indian friends that would spread across most of the American Midwest.

Britain's disrespect angered Adams, but Clay recognized a bluff when he saw one. As a card player, he knew it was a useful deceit, and he told Adams the British were demanding much more than they expected to receive. Adams disagreed, noting in his diary that Clay "has an inconceivable idea."[6]

Clay was proven correct. After the Duke of Wellington defeated Emperor Napoleon Bonaparte of France, Britain lost much of its interest in America for several reasons. First was Wellington's preference for a quick peace treaty. Second was Britain's questionable financial condition. Third was Clay's insistence that any treaty must prevent

Britain from trading with American Indians and encouraging them to rebel. The British worried that France might turn these differences of opinion to their advantage.

Progress, such as it had been, came to a stop. Adams accepted an invitation for the American delegation to visit the British in their lodgings at the Hotel des Pays Bas. The two sides finally met face-to-face on August 8, 1814. The British made absurd demands, the Americans refused, and Clay wondered if Britain's negotiators were stalling.

Trouble at Home

Britain's North American campaign was going well for them. American troops came under fierce gunfire during the British attack on Washington in 1814.

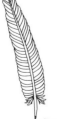

The Duke of Wellington

Wellington led his army against Emperor Napoleon Bonaparte of France in April 1814. Napoleon lost and was exiled to the island of Elba off the coast of Italy. He escaped in February 1815, rejoined his followers, and marched to Paris. On June 18, he met Wellington again at the Battle of Waterloo in Belgium. Wellington quickly ended Napoleon's "Hundred Days of Freedom." Napoleon was exiled to the island of St. Helena, off the African coast, where he died in 1821.

The president and first lady remained in the President's House until forced to leave for their safety. Dolley Madison went to Virginia on August 24 in mid-afternoon and the president followed reluctantly at sunset.[7]

The delays in Ghent, plus worrisome news from America, made the commissioners irritable. Gallatin appointed himself the peacemaker between the other men.[8] Lucretia wrote in August about Clay's reelection to Congress, but the good news did not help to relieve his irritation.

The Americans met daily at 2:00 P.M. and talked until 4:00 P.M. They ate dinner and sat around the table for another two or three hours unless there was something else to do. They went to coffee houses, played cards, attended parties or the theater, and traveled while they waited.

Ending the Battle

Great Britain wanted to resolve the situation so it could attend to other matters. They worried that Russia might side with America. They fretted because their treasury was shrinking. The Duke of Wellington's victory over Napoleon increased his reputation and power, making him a threat.

The duke wanted to end the war in America *status quo ante bellum*. Translated from Latin, this was "the same status as before the war." Wellington's plan meant that, after two miserable years, everything would return to the way it was before the war.

After accomplishing almost nothing for many months, the American and British representatives met for three hours to finalize the terms of the treaty according to Wellington's plan. They examined and signed six copies the next day at the British envoy's residence. The War of 1812 officially ended on December 24, 1814.

All that remained was for both countries to ratify, or approve, the documents. Clay believed the war had ended as well as could be expected. Adams expressed the hope that it might be the last peace treaty ever required between Britain and America.[9]

An evening ceremony of thanksgiving took place in Ghent Cathedral after the treaty was signed. The Americans invited two dozen British and Belgian guests for dinner a few days later. Musicians played the British anthem, "God Save the King," and Britain's Lord Gambier toasted the United States of America. Adams answered with a toast to the British king.

The Americans almost finished their work without another fuss. However, they disagreed over who would safeguard the conference documents and where they should be stored. Clay lobbied for the State Department in Washington. Gallatin preferred London in case any of the commissioners

W. J. Edwards's engraving of Clay was made from a daguerreotype by Mathew Brady. It represented Clay during the period around the signing of the Treaty of Ghent. Clay was in his mid-thirties at the time.

needed them. Adams wanted to keep them until the government told him where to put them. He eventually ignored everyone's advice and took them himself.

Clay's role in the peace conference impressed the British. They understood his determination not to surrender any American soil. He would not sign a treaty that was unfavorable to America's sovereignty or rights. As the only commissioner representing America's expanding West, Clay had held fast to these beliefs throughout the talks.

The Outcome

The War of 1812 brought no significant political gains after two years of fighting, while President Madison endured great stress and trouble at home. However, some doors did remain open for future negotiations. The war had two unexpected results.

First, America's dragging spirits soared as peace approached. Second, the war removed all lingering doubts about the strength of America's economic independence from Britain.[10] Thomas Jefferson wrote from his home in Virginia, "The British war has left us in debt; but that is a cheap price for the good it has done us."[11]

Clay remained in Europe after the treaty was signed. For two weeks, he attended parties and dances hosted by friends and city officials celebrating the end of the war. His schedule allowed time to see Paris and the countryside before going to London for trade talks.

Clay usually resolved personal differences with people before parting company. He bade Adams good-bye and made sure all was well between them before going to Paris. Clay had come to realize that behind Adams's gruff facade was a lonely man. Adams and his wife, Louisa Catherine, did not enjoy a companionable home life. She was regarded as someone who considered herself well above most of society.[12]

To Paris

Clay left by coach at dawn on January 7, 1815. His friend, William Crawford, the new American minister to France, met him in Paris. He had big plans for Clay, starting with a grand tour of the city.

Crawford introduced Clay to many of Europe's most important and influential people within a week of his arrival. Clay was presented to France's King Louis XVIII at the royal palace, known as the Tuileries. King Louis welcomed them and introduced Clay to lords and ladies of his court.

Clay and Crawford dined several times with Madame de Staël, the distinguished French writer. During one visit, she asked Clay if he was aware that Britain had once considered sending the celebrated Duke of Wellington to lead an army against America. Clay was honored that Britain had thought of America as such a worthy foe. Madame surprised him again another day by introducing him to Wellington. She repeated for Wellington what she had told Clay. The nobleman known as the "Iron Duke" laughed and said it would have been "a most notable feather in his cap had he beaten so gallant a people as the Americans."[13]

5

AFTER THE WAR

Clay's visit to Paris passed quickly. His friends teasingly called him Prince Hal, a nickname for Henry, because the French royalty and upper class accepted him so readily. Although Clay had to rely on translators, the French greatly enjoyed his enthusiasm and sense of humor.

Battle of New Orleans

News from America traveled slowly. Clay heard weeks after the fact that British troops had tried to capture New Orleans in early 1815. General Andrew Jackson was unaware of the signed treaty when he led Tennessee and Kentucky sharpshooters into a bloody fight on January 15. The attack was part of the Battle of New Orleans.

Jackson defended the city with volunteer militia. They created a wall of rifle fire between the enemy and their own positions. General Sir Edward Pakenham, the British commanding general, died instantly. Over two thousand of his troops, including veterans of the Napoleonic Wars, were wounded, captured, or killed.[1] The Americans lost only twenty-one men.[2]

Jackson's forces won fame for their relentless fire and their leader became a rising star in the political arena. Others were less impressed because the battle was won after the war had ended. Modern-day Supreme Court Justice Sandra Day O'Connor noted that the battle gave Jackson an "opportunity to make a name for himself."[3]

Jackson harshly criticized the Kentucky militia for failing to capture Britain's Lieutenant Colonel William Thornton and his unit. Jackson claimed that this had happened because they left their posts on the west bank of the Mississippi River. He all but called them cowards. He neglected to mention that his own lack of planning contributed to the problem. Jackson positioned too few men at the site because he had not foreseen a British attack at that site.

Jackson's report on the victory in New Orleans arrived in Washington about the same time as did the Treaty of Ghent. Both events inspired many celebrations. People took immense pride in Britain's humiliating defeat in New Orleans. Americans considered the Treaty of Ghent a signal to the world that the United States was not just an experiment. Britain signed and sent the treaty to Washington, where the Senate ratified it on February 17, 1815.

London

The war's end created a need for trade negotiations to restore business dealings between the United States and Britain. Clay arrived in London on March 21. He and Albert Gallatin went to many parties and dinners, where many people enjoyed Clay's nonstop humor. When someone asked an elderly British nobleman which guest he preferred among so many, he said, "I enjoyed them all, but I liked the Kentucky man best."[4]

John Quincy Adams arrived in London on May 25 to assume his new post as minister to Britain's Court of St. James. He was well informed and eager to begin negotiations. It quickly became apparent that British trade agreements were not like American plans and required many more negotiations.

To everyone's relief, the Americans produced a trade document on May 31 that all present could accept. Adams thought it did little; he signed it, he said, only out of respect for Clay and Gallatin.[5]

Adams had only one firm condition. He insisted the order of the names of the two countries must alternate throughout the document.

The treaty satisfied Clay because it canceled all taxes normally charged for foreign goods. Removing the taxes would reduce the cost of goods and stimulate more trade between America and Britain. Both countries received each other's most favored nation status. Without such status, the countries had paid heavy taxes to buy each other's products. America also joined other approved nations in the profitable trade with British India.

Back to America

The Commercial Convention of 1815 was signed on July 2. Clay and John Payne Todd left London at dawn the next morning for Liverpool to find the next available ship home. Clay warned Todd not to waste time because he was eager to go home.

As it happened, Clay, Todd, Adams, and Gallatin sailed together on July 22. Despite gale winds and heavy seas, they arrived in New York six weeks later on September 1. They were honored for their efforts to end the war and their diplomacy on America's behalf.

Several groups honored Clay in Philadelphia the following week. He received cheers, greetings, congratulations, and gratitude all the way to Lexington.

He was deeply pleased to find that his country considered him a successful statesman at the age of thirty-eight.

He was tired, but happy to be home. He stayed for a couple of months to become reacquainted with his family, review the property, and visit his animals. The children had grown and changed a great deal during his absence.

All the delays in Europe took a serious toll on Clay's finances. His salary and government allowance had not been enough for an unexpectedly long trip. Also, he had had to pay many expenses with his own money. Financial worries prompted him to request more money from the government. He received $27,517.95 in salary and expenses for the eighteen months between January 17, 1814, and July 22, 1815.[6]

Washington

Clay returned to the House of Representatives in late November 1815 and was reelected speaker on December 4. He was glad to be back, although the terrible conditions in Washington shocked him. The whole city seemed to be in shambles. The British assault on August 1814 had severely damaged several buildings, including the President's House, the Capitol, and the Library of Congress.

The library's entire collection of books, maps, and papers were destroyed.

Reconstruction was going to take years and huge sums of money. The Madisons lived at the Octagon House in Washington during the repairs to the President's House.[7] A temporary workplace for Congress was being built. The Senate would use the first floor, and the House would work upstairs.

Dolley Madison

President Madison was nearing the end of his second term and Congress was going to miss his wife, Dolley. She was known with great affection as Lady Presidentess. From the early days of Madison's presidency, in 1809, she hosted social gatherings to advance her husband's goals. She held receptions on Wednesdays in the drawing rooms of the President's House from sundown until nine o'clock.

No invitations were sent and, if enemies encountered one another, she expected them to behave. She combined congressmen with political supporters, government officials, military officers, and businessmen in attractive and relaxed settings. Her parties were formal, but also included entertainment and activities appropriate for the weather.

She transformed the role of the president's wife into that of a public figure so Madison could work behind the scenes without appearing aloof. People

Both Senate and House sessions were considered very exciting events that attracted crowds of spectators. Here, the usual large crowd of visitors listens attentively from the gallery above the Senate floor.

admired her. She realized that many Washington residents were from elsewhere and needed to feel welcome.

Many members of Congress led solely political lives.[8] They lived in boardinghouses during sessions of Congress. They enjoyed companionship and lively conversation with fellow politicians at dinner. Most houses accepted men from all political parties, but some preferred that all residents be of the same party.

Henry Clay was among Dolley Madison's favorite friends. She met him in 1810 as his political star was rising. Government business often paused briefly when she brought friends to the House to hear Clay speak. Other women with political interests followed her example. They watched House and Senate proceedings from the upper balconies.

Some people viewed Congressional sessions as social events. Others considered them opportunities to listen, learn, and take notes to share with others. Margaret Bayard Smith, the wife of Senator Samuel Smith of Maryland, wrote to a friend that, after Clay spoke, he came to "sit a few minutes on the steps with me . . . to discuss the speech."[9] Smith described another lively House session as being "as good as going to a play, but here all the characters are real."[10]

6

SPEAKER OF THE HOUSE

The physical damage in Washington, D.C., symbolized bigger problems facing the nation. America's relations with Spain were in jeopardy again when Clay returned to the House of Representatives in November 1815.

Spanish Florida

American Indian raiding parties had been attacking parts of Georgia for years. They dashed out of Spanish Florida to terrify Georgia residents. They stole whatever they could find and retreated to safety in Florida's thick, swampy terrain. The situation improved a little after General Jackson arrived in October 1813. He led 2,500 Tennessee volunteers to avenge the bloody massacre of 250 white settlers at Fort Mims in Georgia.[1] The U.S. Army compound was in the Mississippi Territory, not far from Spanish Florida.

In March 1814, Jackson defeated the Creek and their leader, Chief Red Eagle. The general led his forces to victory on the Tallapoosa River in the Battle of Horseshoe Bend. The Treaty of Fort Jackson included stiff penalties for the Creek. They were required to give 23 million acres of land to the United States.[2] Many escaped into Florida to await another opportunity to attack.

Jackson's forces encountered American Indians again in 1817. The Seminole and a band of runaway slaves, also from Florida, had been raiding settlements and killing Americans for years.

After the Alabama Territory was created in 1819, President Monroe realized Spain did not intend to do anything about the American Indian raids. He ordered Jackson into action with a stern warning not to enter Spanish Florida unless he was following an identifiable enemy.

Jackson immediately exceeded his orders. During the First Seminole War, he chased slaves and American Indians across the Florida border. Jackson's troops destroyed various settlements at Pensacola and St. Marks. They routed the Spanish governor's troops and torched Seminole villages.[3]

The general executed two British citizens, Robert Ambrister and Alexander Arbuthnot, for plotting with the Seminole. Americans worried that the deaths could lead to war with the British.[4] Great Britain was highly displeased, but it did not attempt to retaliate. Because Spain feared that it would lose Florida to America without any compensation, the Spanish began to consider selling the territory.

The Adams-Onis Treaty

Jackson's daring had thrilled many Americans and upset others, including Clay. Spain's minister to the United States, Luis de Onis, demanded an apology and insisted that Jackson be punished. Monroe's cabinet wanted to censure, or punish, the general to show their strong disapproval of his attacks. Clay, as speaker of the house, agreed completely. Jackson's only defender was John Quincy Adams. As secretary of state, Adams told Minister de Onis there would be no censure. He added that Spain could either surrender East Florida or send an army to defend it.

Adams and Onis signed the Adams-Onis Treaty on February 22, 1819. Congress ratified it two days later. The treaty provided $5 million to cover claims for property damage that Americans believed were caused by the Spanish. In other treaty provisions, Spain gave up all claims to the Oregon Territory, and the Sabine River became a permanent border between the United States and Spain's southwestern territory. Spain also gave the United States land that includes present-day Florida and parts of present-day Alabama and Mississippi.

The Panic of 1819

Relieved that war had been avoided, Americans began to pay more attention to their personal lives. They enjoyed expensive European products again. People bought large sections of public lands. (At that time, public lands were areas owned by the government that were available for purchase.) Property values began to rise, and owners received their deeds when the land was paid for in full.

However, people throughout the country began to have money problems. Banks contributed to the country's economic trouble. They kept poor business records, full of mistakes and incomplete entries. They were not always sure of their clients' financial health; major problems surfaced when people realized they could not pay all their debts.

As people lost money, they could buy fewer and fewer items. Jobs became scarce and soon thousands of people were out of work. This period of economic troubles was called the Panic of 1819. The economy worsened as the panic began to affect the whole country. Business activity dropped further as the Second Bank of the United States called in outstanding loans and changed its credit policies. The bank began lending less money and charging higher interest rates. People were afraid they could lose everything.

Treasury Secretary William Crawford asked Congress to consider debt relief for people in distress. It approved his proposal to extend the time allowed to pay for public lands from four to eight years. Crawford also offered citizens a choice that involved dividing a troubled property. The owner could keep the portion he had paid for and abandon the rest without paying a penalty.

As the Panic of 1819 continued, Clay's rivalry with Jackson became more intense. About all they had in common was that both were from what was considered "the West" at the time. (Clay was from Kentucky, and Jackson was from Tennessee.) They were polite to each other when necessary, but otherwise neither had anything to say unless they were arguing.

Clay gave a speech in the House on January 20, 1819, condemning Jackson's actions in the First Seminole War. Clay also criticized President James Monroe and Secretary of State John Quincy Adams.[5] Congress rejected Clay's view that Jackson had been too severe. Jackson never forgot or forgave Clay's public insults.[6]

The Missouri Territory

The Missouri Territory was a part of the Louisiana Purchase. It had been settled by many Southerners, who had brought their slaves with them. Missouri was the first area entirely west of the Mississippi River to apply for statehood. It did not have a river or other natural boundary to indicate its borderline between the North and the South. Slavery was an issue for admission to the Union because about ten thousand slaves lived in the Missouri Territory.

In early 1819, Congress began debating the Missouri Enabling Act that would admit the territory into the Union as a slave state. Every state had two senators, each with one vote, but the House membership was based on the size of each state's population. Also, Southern states counted 60 percent of their slaves in their population. Many people worried that if Missouri became a state, it would tip the Senate's delicate balance of power between Free States and slave states.

The Missouri Compromise of 1820

The Missouri Enabling Act of 1819 highlighted many long-standing political and social problems. Angry voters wrote to their congressmen, who were arguing among themselves. As speaker of the house, Henry Clay juggled all of the viewpoints. He personally believed slavery would disappear if slaves were allowed to return to Africa.

On February 13, 1819, Representative James Tallmadge, Jr., of New York proposed an amendment to the Missouri Enabling Act to prohibit bringing additional slaves into Missouri. It also

The American Colonization Society

Henry Clay helped found an organization in 1816 that was designed to move free African Americans to a new colony in Africa. The group was called the American Colonization Society (ACS). It was very controversial. Clay and others argued that they were trying to help the free African Americans by letting them move back to their country of origin on a voluntarily basis. However, opponents believed that the society only helped slavery since many slave owners felt that free African Americans stirred up unrest amongst the slaves.

The ACS's settlement was named Monrovia after President James Monroe. The first African Americans arrived there in 1822. In 1838, Monrovia became part of the country Liberia. However, the society's effort ultimately failed. By 1860, only between eleven and twelve thousand African Americans had moved to the settlement. Clay and the other founders had not considered that most free African Americans had been born in the United States. They did not want to move to a land with which they were unfamiliar.

required that slaves born in the Missouri Territory be freed when they reached the age of twenty-five. Northern legislators passed the amendment over Southern objections, with a vote of 79 to 67. The Senate defeated it by a vote of 31 to 7.

When Congress reconvened in late 1819, the district of Maine wanted to split off from Massachusetts. Maine's citizens wanted to enter the Union as a Free State.[7] The admission of both Maine and Missouri would maintain the delicate balance between Free States and slave states in the Senate.

On February 16, 1820, the Senate decided to bundle the Missouri Enabling Act and the Maine bill together into one piece of legislation. Senator Jesse B. Thomas of Illinois proposed and the Senate accepted one change to the bill. His amendment banned slavery from the Louisiana Purchase Territory north of latitude 36° 30' North.

Many representatives would not consider or even discuss the combined bill. They argued about every proposed solution. Clay was exhausted from trying to get members to compromise. In late February, he finally found twenty-three House members and seven carefully chosen senators who were willing to discuss the problem.

The committee reported on March 2, urging Congress to accept the Senate measure with only one change. The members strongly advised dividing the bundled Missouri and Maine bills into three parts. They wanted separate votes for: a free Maine; a slave Missouri; and restriction of slaves north of latitude 36° 30', except for Missouri. Agreement finally was reached after months of argument. Every congressman could vote his personal preference on each issue. This agreement was called the Missouri Compromise.

On March 3, Clay had another victory. He cleverly outwitted an old foe, Congressman John Randolph of Virginia, who did not support the Missouri Compromise. Clay postponed further discussion of the issue until the following day. When

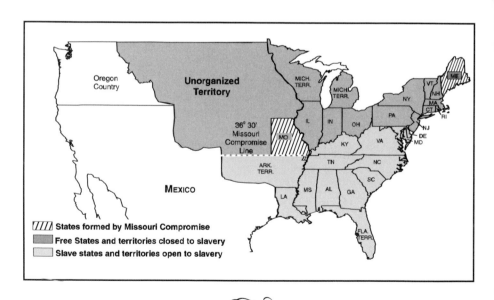

Henry Clay's Missouri Compromise of 1820 provided a temporary solution to the slavery debate between the North and South.

Randolph moved to reopen the subject, Clay replied that he had signed the Missouri Compromise bill and sent it to the Senate. He added that it could not be recalled.

President James Monroe signed the Missouri Compromise on March 6, 1820. A little over a week later, on March 15, Maine joined the Union as a Free State. The president also allowed Missouri to prepare a state constitution. Missouri became the Union's twenty-fourth state on March 10, 1821, entering as a slave state. The equal balance between the Free States and slave states had been preserved.

The Great Compromiser

Henry Clay had done a great service to the country. Modern-day Supreme Court Justice Sandra Day O'Connor commented that he "postponed for many years the confrontation on the issue of slavery in the territories."[8] Clay's management of very difficult legislation and his efforts to satisfy as many people as possible earned him great respect and the title, "The Great Compromiser."

Not every citizen was pleased with the Missouri Compromise. Former President Thomas Jefferson took a longer view. Fearing that it would not last, he said, "This momentous question, like a fire-bell in the night, awakened and filled me with terror. I considered it at once the knell of the union. It is hushed, indeed . . . But this is a reprieve only, not a final sentence . . ."[9]

Clay left the House after the Missouri Compromise became law. He was exhausted and unwell. His lagging law practice required attention. His family and friends still owed large sums for loans made to them during the Panic of 1819. He also owed money for debts incurred in long-past poker games. Ashland needed repairs. Clay knew he must tend to business at home.

Henry Clay needed peace and quiet with Lucretia and the children. He resigned as speaker, but remained in the House while he considered his future.

7

THE CLAYS AT ASHLAND

The Clays left Washington, D.C., in March 1821, traveling by train, steamboat, and carriage through wet, wintry weather. They were glad to be home at the end of the third week.

Ashland was no longer the cottage on a few acres that Clay had bought in 1806. During the following five years, he added pieces of surrounding land until he owned a plantation with more than four hundred acres of pastures and woods. Clay demolished the original house in 1809 and over the next two years built a large two-story brick home. His son Henry, Jr., liked to say he was "born in the dining room of the house."[1]

The Family

The Clays had nine living children in 1821. Their five sons ranged from the infant, John Morrison, to nineteen-year-old Theodore, with Thomas, Henry, Jr., and James in between. Their four daughters were Anne, Susan, Lucretia, and Eliza. The couple had lost Laura and Henrietta in their first years of life.[2]

Henry loved his children, but he was not an attentive father. He was away too much to know them well. Lucretia supervised their education, discipline, and training. She had the help of servants, but the lively children sometimes overwhelmed her.

Once, when Clay was gone for a long period, Lucretia learned of a young man, said by local citizens to be "solitary and poor . . . ill of a fever in a hotel in town."[3] His name was Amos Kendall and he was a graduate of Dartmouth College in New Hampshire.

Lucretia brought him to Ashland and nursed him back to health. When she discovered his background, she asked if he would tutor the children. She offered him three hundred dollars a year. He agreed to stay six months out of gratitude for her care during his illness. He was to improve the children's education and firmly discipline their behavior. They were smart, but without manners. Whether they neglected their assignments, or paid

little attention in class, they were far behind in their studies.

Kendall had serious contests of wills with the unruly boys. They finally gave in after a few months. The girls also cooperated once they knew what Kendall expected. He was able to bring them to their proper levels of learning. They grasped his lessons well, if and when they tried. Kendall was satisfied with their progress after one year, at which time he resigned his post.

Lucretia

Lucretia's trips to Washington, D.C., and back to Kentucky required up to three months, depending

This picture depicts Ashland as it appeared shortly after it was rebuilt between 1809 and 1811. Over four hundred acres of woods and meadows surrounded the house.

on the weather. She liked the capital's lovely spring and fall days, but humid summers and gloomy winters were not for her. She made friends while Clay worked most of the time. Lucretia enjoyed the many parties and dinners they attended. However, she had no interest in the latest Washington gossip.

Margaret Bayard Smith, the wife of Senator Samuel Smith of Maryland, became her closest friend. She observed that Lucretia was "a thousand times better pleased, sitting in the room with all her children round her and a pile of work by her side, than in the most brilliant drawing room."[4]

Lucretia was happiest at Ashland with her family and lifelong friends. When Clay was away, she kept busy with the family, visitors, her home, the plantation, and its workers. She was a good money manager. When Clay returned after a long absence, she often returned the check he had left her for household expenses.

For extra money, Lucretia sold Ashland's milk, butter, and cured hams to friends and neighbors. She also worked with Ashland's manager, who oversaw the crops and about a dozen slaves who lived on and worked the grounds.

The Farmer

Clay experimented with various crops of tobacco, corn, wheat, and rye when he was home. He crossbred the lush Kentucky grasses that kept his animals healthy. He worked to improve the livestock, including hogs, horses, goats, mules, sheep, cows, and cattle.

Among Clay's favorite animals were his Hereford cattle. He first saw the breed in 1814 while he was in Europe discussing the Treaty of Ghent. He often traveled when the negotiations were delayed. On one such occasion, he attended the Royal Smithfield Show in Britain. The Hereford cattle at the show delighted him so much that he arranged for two bulls and two cows to be shipped to Ashland. They were the first of their breed imported into the United States.

Racehorses were Clay's favorite and most expensive animals. He loved the excitement of racing, the variety of people involved, and betting on the outcome. He began breeding racehorses well before 1806. That year, he and some friends formed a partnership. They bought a stallion named Buzzard. Buzzard had several offspring before he died two years later. Clay's horses eventually won enough races to pay for a private track at Ashland.

Clay became a gentleman farmer with a pro-West outlook. He loved life far from Washington's troubles and pressures. He even considered leaving politics for good. He once wrote to a friend, "My attachment to rural occupation [farm work] every day acquires more strength, and if it continues . . . I shall be fully prepared to renounce forever the strifes [troubles] of public life."[5]

Back to Washington

Clay stayed at Ashland through one term, which was enough for him to realize that he enjoyed political life too much to give it up. Kentucky voters returned him to the House in 1822. His health was poor through the fall. He became ill during a business trip to Ohio. When he developed a high fever, a local doctor advised him not to travel until he recovered completely. Due to false information, the Washington *National Intelligencer* reported his death. After he recovered, Clay notified friends that "word of his demise was premature."[6]

Congress convened on March 3, 1823, and reelected him as speaker. The family received other welcome news in the next few months. Clay's ceaseless efforts during the two-year absence from Congress had revived his law practice. The family's finances had been rescued.

Clay had been the lawyer for the Bank of the United States in Ohio and Kentucky for many years after the Panic of 1819. He gradually came to dislike collecting money owed to the bank and suing people who did not pay. He sometimes had to take them to court to collect whatever funds they had, even if that left them penniless.

Clay was paid well, but those who lost their homes and property bore him a deep resentment. The situation grew worse as Kentucky's economy declined because it could not compete with other regions or with foreign imports.

The American System

His uncomfortable position spurred Clay to revive a financial plan he had worked on for years. He called it the American System. It had the following components:

1. A strong national bank to serve as the country's financial center;
2. A network of toll roads and canals funded by the federal government for transportation to inland states and the West;
3. Heavy taxes on European imports to help American goods compete with less costly foreign products; and
4. Return to the states all moneys made from selling public lands.

After spending years refining his plan, Clay submitted it to Congress in March 1824 in one large block instead of several small ones. He was very disappointed when the members showed no interest

This well-known picture of Henry Clay, called "Father of the American System," was painted by John Neagle in the 1840s.

in it. They turned their attention to what they felt were more pressing matters.

Clay also had a very different experience in 1824. The national caucus that had chosen presidential candidates for years was no longer functional. There were no well-organized political parties. Each region had a favorite candidate and the Kentucky Legislature nominated Clay. He accepted, although he knew that winning would be hard. He knew his position with the Bank of the United States could be an obstacle.

Election of 1824

Four presidential candidates ran in 1824. They were Secretary of State John Quincy Adams of Massachusetts, Treasury Secretary William H. Crawford of Georgia, General Andrew Jackson of Tennessee, and Representative Henry Clay of Kentucky.

No candidate won a majority of the electoral votes. Under the Twelfth Amendment to the U.S. Constitution, the top three candidates could remain in the race. They were Jackson, Adams, and Crawford. Clay placed fourth and was eliminated, but remained speaker of the House. The election then went to the House of Representatives for resolution. The Constitution allowed Clay to give any electoral votes he received to another candidate.

John Quincy Adams and Henry Clay met privately during the evening of January 9, 1825. Adams, who usually wrote detailed entries in his personal diary, did not record their conversation.

On February 9, each state's delegation cast their electoral votes for a favorite candidate. The Kentucky Legislature instructed Clay to vote for Andrew Jackson, but he did not. Clay knew that many Kentucky residents bitterly resented Jackson for having accused their militia of cowardice ten years earlier in the Battle of New Orleans.[7]

The House selected Adams on the first ballot with a bare majority of thirteen votes, some due to Clay's support. Jackson took seven votes and Crawford received four. When the results reached Adams's father, John Adams, the former president said, "No man who ever held the office of President would congratulate a friend on obtaining it."[8]

Secretary of State

Within five days after the election, Adams appointed Clay his secretary of state. In the past, the cabinet post had been a potential step toward the presidency.

Crawford's supporters objected loudly. They believed Clay and Adams had made an illegal agreement that protesters called a "corrupt bargain." The phrase was heard everywhere. Jackson supporters also believed Adams and Clay had conspired to prevent their man from becoming president.[9] The general became even more embittered toward Clay.

Clay's health varied throughout 1825. He spent much of the spring preparing to move his family to Washington. Lucretia was not happy, but they had no choice. Clay's cabinet post would not allow for long round-trips to Kentucky.

Tragedy

The Clays left Lexington in late July after renting out Ashland and selling or auctioning furnishings and animals. Clay even parted with his Hereford cattle. As the Clays neared Cincinnati, Ohio, twelve-year-old Eliza developed a high fever. Her parents thought it might be due to all the changes in her life, and they continued their trip. When Eliza became very ill, a doctor said she should not travel until she recovered.

Lucretia stayed with her while Clay continued to Washington. Within twenty miles of the capital, he read in the *National Intelligencer* that Eliza had died on August 11.[10] He was overcome with guilt for leaving Lucretia to go through the ordeal alone.[11]

Misfortune struck again six weeks later. The Clays' daughter, Susan, died of yellow fever on September 18 at her home in New Orleans. She was twenty years old. She was survived by her husband, a toddler, and an infant. Lucretia was crushed to lose her bright, cheerful young daughter who had planned to visit her in Washington.

The Clays lodged at Emily Clark's boarding-house in Washington until they could find a home. In mid-October, they rented Richard Forest's three-story brick house near the Capitol. Lucretia's religion helped her while she grieved for her daughters. Clay buried himself in endless, boring paperwork until the stress of his job brought him close to a breakdown.

President Adams worried about Clay's exhaustion and bad cough. He noted in his diary that Clay's "health is so infirm that he told me . . . he [might have to] resign."[12] The two had not been friends in earlier days. However, their new positions helped them to agree on policies and programs. Recalling his own exhaustion while secretary of state, Adams encouraged Clay to work at his own pace. If Clay felt too ill to attend meetings, Adams came to his home. This new understanding helped them put aside past problems and work together.

8

WASHINGTON POLITICS

Clay received two attacks on his character in the spring of 1826. The first came from the pro-Jackson *United States Telegraph* newspaper, accusing him of dirty tricks and dishonesty.[1] Clay did not respond to the charges.

The second attack was more personal. A long-time rival, John Randolph of Roanoke, Virginia, insulted him in the Senate by mentioning the "corrupt bargain" charge. Clay responded by challenging Randolph to a duel.

General Thomas Jesup, Clay's second, or assistant, made the arrangements. Dueling had old rituals involving formality and polite language. These were unrelated to the duel's potential for injury and death. The Clays' friends, Samuel and Margaret Smith, visited the couple the evening before the duel. They were surprised to find Lucretia calm and seemingly unaware of it.

A Duel

On Saturday, April 8, 1826, at 4:30 in the afternoon, Clay met Randolph at Little Falls bridge near the Potomac River in Virginia.[2] As their seconds reviewed details, Randolph's pistol fired accidentally. Clay ignored the shot. The two men stepped off ten paces, turned, and faced each other. At Jesup's signal, both fired one round and missed. Clay's bullet hit a rock and Randolph's shell nicked a tree. Clay declined when Randolph's second asked to halt the duel.

Round two went the same way. Clay scattered dirt while Randolph fired into the distance. Randolph called as he approached, "I do not fire at you, Mr. Clay. I give you my hand." He added, laughing, "You owe me a coat." Indeed, Randolph's garment had the raggedy threads of a very recent bullet hole near the waist. Clay replied, "I am glad the debt is no greater."[3]

Election of 1828

Clay ran for president in 1828 as the National Republican party candidate. He promoted his own campaign. He traveled when his work allowed, addressing huge crowds in Virginia, Maryland, Kentucky, Ohio, and Indiana.

Jackson won by a two-to-one margin and the tough campaign left Clay exhausted. On his way to and from home, he spent a few days relaxing in the warm mineral baths at White Sulphur Springs, Virginia.

After his inauguration in March 1829, Jackson rode his big gray horse to President's House. Throngs of well-wishers were still arriving long after he had gone to his lodgings at Gadsby's Hotel.[4] The kitchen staff placed tubs of punch around the lawn to draw people out of the crowded house. Margaret Bayard Smith told friends, "The noisy and disorderly rabble . . . brought to my mind . . . the mobs in the Tuileries [during the French Revolution]."[5]

Clay retired when his term as secretary of state ended in early 1829. He was depressed about losing the election to Jackson. However, he tried to hide his physical and emotional pain. Margaret Bayard Smith visited the family and she was shocked by Clay's appearance. She wrote to a friend that "he was much thinner, very pale . . . his voice was feeble and mournful."[6]

Clay called on John Quincy Adams. They had a friendly parting. He told the former president that he hoped to hear from him. Adams wanted to show his appreciation for all that Clay had tried to do as secretary of state. He offered a Supreme Court appointment. Clay declined with thanks. He told Adams he was going to Ashland to restore his health and spirits. The campaign had been so brutal that he wanted to be away from Washington during Jackson's presidency.

About one hundred guests honored the Clays and wished them well at a dinner party in the Mansion Hotel before their departure. Clay enjoyed seeing little inns and other signs of progress along the way to Kentucky. They indicated that more Americans were moving westward.

Home Again

As he had promised, Clay returned to Transylvania University and joined the Board of Directors. He advised the president and interviewed prospective teachers. He also offered faculty and board members the services of his law office, and he became Transylvania's spokesman in the East.

The Clays relaxed until their belongings arrived in two wagons. Ashland required only routine repairs. Clay celebrated the family's homecoming by building an ice house. The plantation was Clay's retreat, his peaceful haven. It had always revived him after difficult sessions in Washington.

The rear view of Ashland has a large grassy area like the ones the Clays used for parties and outdoor dining in summer. Clay often walked the length of the long oval path that looped the grounds.

A Great Race

Clay owned Woodpecker, a horse that many owners and jockeys considered Kentucky's finest stallion. Clay also owned Woodpecker's mother and had owned his prize-winning grandfather, the great Buzzard. Clay especially enjoyed Woodpecker's match race with Collier, a prize stallion of Virginia. A huge crowd arrived early on race day to picnic and discuss horses.

Clay's horse and jockey wore Ashland's blue and yellow racing silks. Woodpecker and Collier were in peak condition and prancing with excitement. The contest began and both stallions galloped quickly around the four-mile course. The crowd roared as the horses flew past the finish line a few minutes later. Woodpecker's record remained unbroken. His owner was very proud.

Clay enjoyed the business side of owning horses. He carefully recorded details of their births, health, diet, and medical information. He and other owners throughout the East, South, and Kentucky often shared information about bloodlines, specific animals, and events.

The Clay Boys

Clay was extremely proud of Henry, Jr., an outstanding West Point cadet. He and his younger brothers, James and John, were Clay's hopes for the future. However, the older sons, Thomas and Theodore, were another story. They had no goals, discipline, or jobs. They were uncooperative, ill-tempered complainers with big debts.

Back to Washington

Clay occasionally spoke to groups at Ashland on a variety of subjects. In March 1829, he told his listeners, "Government is a trust, and the officers of the government are trustees; and both the trust and the trustees are created for the benefit of the people."[7]

Clay expected Jackson to bungle his presidency and destroy any chance for a second term in 1832. He believed that after Jackson was gone, New England and the mid-Atlantic states should join forces with the growing West. Mutual cooperation would bring both regions more business and political strength. The West needed roads, canals, and other internal improvements.

On November 18, 1831, Kentucky's Legislature elected Clay to fill a vacancy in the U.S. Senate, beginning March 4, 1832. Jackson's most outspoken critic was about to become leader of the opposition in Congress. Henry Clay welcomed the challenge.

The Second Bank of the United States

Serious problems had arisen prior to the presidential election of 1832. One involved the Second Bank of the United States. The bank had been given a business charter when it opened in 1816. The renewal of the document was due in 1836.

Clay supported the bank for many reasons. Most vital was its role in providing funds to support the federal government. Clay had worked through the years with many people who owed money to banks. He knew the nation would suffer a severe crisis if banks were to demand full payment for all

Andrew Jackson (pictured) was Clay's biggest foe before and after he became president. More than just political enemies, they could not even manage to be friends.

outstanding loans and then close their doors. Clay could not forget the years of struggle after the Panic of 1819, when so many families lost everything.

President Jackson strongly opposed the Second Bank of the United States. He thought it had too much control over America's money supply. He also was suspicious of the eastern financial community. He believed rich people used the bank to increase their own wealth. He was sure average citizens lacked such opportunities because they had little or no money to invest.

Clay persuaded Nicholas Biddle, the bank's director, to apply to renew the charter in 1832, four years ahead of schedule. Clay wanted the bank to become a major issue in the fall election. He expected Jackson's actions regarding the bank to hurt the president's reputation. Congress approved the renewal, but Jackson vetoed it on July 10. He ended Clay's scheme when he transferred $11 million in government deposits from the bank to various state-owned banks. Jackson's enemies referred to them as "pet banks."

Election of 1832

Henry Clay was healthy enough to run for president in 1832, but the office escaped him again. Jackson won by more than 157,000 popular votes and took 219 electoral votes to Clay's 49. The electoral count was a mortifying defeat for the senator. He was so upset that he even considered resigning from the Senate.

The Nullification Crisis

A serious problem had occurred several months earlier that affected the election. South Carolina's legislature voted in early 1832 to nullify, or disregard, a moderate tax bill Jackson had signed into law.

For almost two decades, tariffs had gradually become America's second most controversial issue, after slavery. The South was vulnerable because it had few manufacturers and had to depend on goods made elsewhere. Some came from large manufacturing centers in the North; others were from Europe and Asia. When America applied high tariffs to foreign imports, other countries taxed American exports at equally high rates.

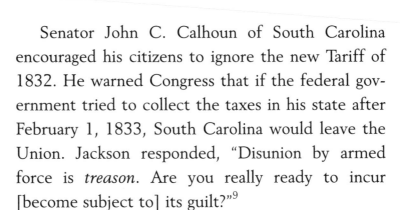

The Tariff of Abominations
Congress passed a very unpopular bill in 1828 during Adams's presidency. It protected New England manufacturers from foreign competition by adding high taxes, or tariffs, to the price of imported products. The new tariff was especially helpful in Ohio, New York, Pennsylvania and Kentucky, where Jackson's political support was the most weak.[8] Angry Southerners called the despised bill the Tariff of Abominations.

Senator John C. Calhoun of South Carolina encouraged his citizens to ignore the new Tariff of 1832. He warned Congress that if the federal government tried to collect the taxes in his state after February 1, 1833, South Carolina would leave the Union. Jackson responded, "Disunion by armed force is *treason*. Are you really ready to incur [become subject to] its guilt?"[9]

The president threatened to send federal troops to collect the tariffs. South Carolina's residents were furious. After many huddles and meetings, Henry Clay produced the Compromise Tariff of 1833, which was acceptable to both Jackson and the South. It called for the gradual lowering of tariff rates. The Senate passed Clay's bill, along with a force bill that authorized the military to collect South Carolina's taxes if necessary. That state

The Great Triumvirate

Congressmen achieved a certain celebrity status after 1814. Henry Clay and his colleagues, Daniel Webster of Massachusetts and John C. Calhoun of South Carolina, became the celebrated threesome known as the "Great Triumvirate."

Each of the three men used his unique style of speaking to convey his message. Calhoun's ability to persuade was a product of his brilliant mind and straightforward, common-sense judgment. Webster's talent for commanding undivided attention was due to his wide vocabulary of rich, descriptive language. Henry Clay captured allies and opponents alike with his deep voice and dramatic gestures. He knew his mannerisms were effective and used them to his best advantage.

When Clay resigned from the Senate in 1842, he apologized to his colleagues for sometimes speaking impolitely in the chamber. He also admitted that he could not always keep his temper under control. On these occasions, he had used "language offensive and susceptible of ungracious interpretation toward my brother senators."[10] Such occasions may have been what prompted Senator John C. Calhoun to say, "I don't like Clay. He is a bad man, an imposter, a creator of wicked schemes. I wouldn't speak to him, but, by God, I love him!"[11]

stayed in the Union because the tariff had been lowered to its satisfaction.

President Van Buren

Martin Van Buren was elected president in 1836. He was Jackson's hand-picked successor and the first president born in the United States. Those who preceded him were British subjects born before the Declaration of Independence. Although Clay and Van Buren had prickly political relations, they enjoyed a warm personal friendship. Clay liked to tease Van Buren, who seldom understood the joke. This made Clay's remarks even more amusing to others.

On one occasion, the President's House laundry room caught fire. Several people, including Clay, hurried to help. He encountered Van Buren in the hallway and was told everything was fine. Clay grasped the president's hand and whispered loudly, "We want you out of the White House, Mr. Van Buren, but we don't want you *burnt* out!"[12]

What little humor Van Buren did possess vanished with the Panic of 1837 and a deep financial depression. Clay blamed the serious situation on eight years of Jackson's poor financial policies. Clay constantly had warned that Jackson did not attend to the nation's economy enough. America slid into a period of financial peril that lasted for years.

9

A NATION AT WAR

M any Whigs urged Clay not to run for president in 1840. They believed he had too many political enemies. Also, he had already lost two presidential races. Therefore, the Whig Party chose William Henry Harrison as their candidate instead of Henry Clay.

President Harrison

Harrison, a sixty-seven-year-old military hero, was the son of Benjamin Harrison, a signer of the Declaration of Independence. Clay was very disappointed not to receive the Whig nomination.[1] However, he campaigned for Harrison and even spoke in Nashville, Tennessee, Andrew Jackson's hometown.

Clay had good reasons for supporting Harrison. He believed he and his fellow congressmen could use their positions to control Harrison's political plans. After his election victory, the incoming president stopped at Ashland on his way to Washington.[2] He offered Clay any cabinet post in his administration and encouraged him to accept secretary of state. Clay declined with thanks.[3] Later, Harrison chose Senator Daniel Webster of Massachusetts for the position.

At his inauguration, Harrison stood on the Capitol steps for two hours in cold, windy weather without a hat or coat. Within days, he developed lung congestion that progressed to pneumonia. Harrison died at the President's House on April 4, 1840, one month after taking office. He was the oldest man to become president up until that time, the last born under British rule, and the first to die in office. With the death of Harrison, Clay lost a president who would have supported his efforts in Congress.[4]

President Tyler

Vice-President John Tyler of Virginia succeeded Harrison. Tyler understood political systems, but he has not been considered a strong leader by most historians. He did not offer Clay a position in his administration. Because Tyler became president due to Harrison's death, his critics nicknamed him "His Accidency."

Clay often clashed with the president. After one encounter, Tyler exploded, "Go you now then, Mr. Clay, to your end of the avenue . . . and there perform your duty to the country as you think proper. . . . I shall do mine at this end . . . as I shall think proper."[5]

Tyler's Troubles

A few months into Tyler's term, Clay sponsored a bill in the Senate to establish a new national bank. It would replace the Second Bank of the United States that closed after Jackson did not renew its charter in 1832.

Clay's bill included a statement of the bank's right to establish branches in the states, even if they were not wanted. The issue caused many arguments in Congress. Although both Tyler and Clay were Whigs, Tyler vetoed the Fiscal Bank bill on August 16, 1840. His decision was most unpopular and an angry mob gathered outside the President's House that night. They burned Tyler in effigy in the most violent protest at the mansion up to that time.[6]

Tyler's action deeply angered his Cabinet. Five out of six members agreed to resign starting at forty-eight hours after Tyler's veto. They did so at one-hour intervals, starting at noon on Saturday,

September 11. The last man resigned at five o'clock. The president's son and private secretary, John, recorded the exact minute that each man submitted his resignation. The sixth Cabinet member, Daniel Webster, remained with the president.

Tyler's mishandling of the bank bill caused him to be drummed out of the Whig Party. Two days after the Cabinet members resigned, a real drum was used in the "removal ceremony" in the Capitol yard. Tyler was declared a president without a political party.[7] The Whigs in Congress made his life miserable in the following months by refusing to approve almost all his Cabinet choices.

Preparing for 1844

Clay resigned from the Senate on March 31, 1842, and returned to private life. Tyler had not supported his efforts, which was a big disappointment. Clay needed to see matters from another perspective far from Washington. He decided to go home, organize his personal affairs, and prepare for another presidential campaign in 1844. He intended to divide his time between practicing law and visiting the people of Kentucky to hear their views.

Clay and Van Buren believed they would be the presidential candidates in 1844 because no party would support Tyler's reelection. Therefore, they met at Ashland in late April to make plans.

They agreed not to discuss the possibility of annexing Texas during the campaign.[8]

Van Buren did not clearly pick a side in his public announcement regarding annexation. He said that, while he might favor it someday, he wanted to wait until Mexico accepted the idea of Texas as part of the United States.[9] His attempt to appear neutral failed because Democrats were excited about expanding to new territories. At the Democratic Convention in Baltimore, Maryland, they chose Speaker of the House James K. Polk of Tennessee to be their presidential candidate.

The idea of Texas fascinated the public. Southerners, including Tyler and Polk, recognized the financial benefits the territory would bring to the South. They envisioned great stretches of open land. New cotton fields would require more slaves.

Annexation of Texas

Texas had gained independence from Mexico in 1836. Congress passed a resolution admitting the Republic of Texas into the Union in 1844. President Tyler signed it on March 1, 1845, three days before leaving office. Southerners saw annexation as a way to increase their lands, crops, and slaves. Many Northerners feared the Texas Territory would be divided into four or five slave states and reduce their influence in Congress.

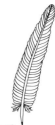

The Constitution's "three-fifths rule" for counting slaves would increase the number of voters. Texas could become a political giant.

Many Northerners worried about the same issues from the opposite point of view. They feared that annexing Texas would reduce their share of the total population and, therefore, their political influence. They believed a larger slave population would bring major problems and perhaps even armed conflict.

Although Clay owned slaves, he believed that all slaves should be freed gradually. However, he felt that only the states, not the federal government, had the right to free slaves. Clay also thought that slave owners should be paid for freed slaves.

Clay's long-held position on slavery satisfied neither Northern nor Southern voters. His views were confusing to them. Some accused him of saying whatever people wanted to hear.

If the United States decided to annex the Texas Territory, the South would gain great political power. Clay worried about problems like this and the fact that the Republic of Texas owed the United States a $13 million debt. Someone would have to pay it. Clay did not want hardworking Americans to bear that burden.

President Tyler returned to private life at the end of his term. He cleared the way for James K. Polk, who shared two of Tyler's goals, annexing Texas and foiling Henry Clay's presidential aspirations.

President Polk

During the campaign, Whig supporters at political rallies chanted, "Who is James K. Polk?" Though Polk was a former congressman and one-term governor of Tennessee, he was a "dark horse" in the

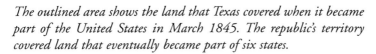

The outlined area shows the land that Texas covered when it became part of the United States in March 1845. The republic's territory covered land that eventually became part of six states.

James Knox Polk defeated Clay for the presidency in 1844. The Mexican war took its toll on Polk, who aged a great deal during his single term in office.

election. The term *dark horse* refers to a candidate who is relatively unknown and not expected to win an election. The Democrats chose Polk because they could not agree on more well-known candidates.

The Democrats used the slogan "Fifty-four Forty or Fight" in the presidential campaign of 1844. It described their plan to move the Oregon Territory's northern border from 42° North latitude to 54° 40' North latitude. This would give America a large amount of Great Britain's land in Canada.

Clay's humor charmed audiences while Polk spoke seriously about the issues. Clay took 48 percent of the popular vote, but an odd political quirk cost him the election.

James Birney of New York was the Liberty party candidate. Birney's only issue was antislavery. He drew few votes from across the nation. However, he took enough away from Clay in New York to give

James K. Polk the state's electoral votes and the presidency. Polk won the popular vote by a margin of thirty-eight thousand votes out of 2.7 million cast.

Clay was devastated. He had been sure he would win. People sent hundreds of beautiful, expensive gifts. A steady stream of visitors reminded him that he had many supporters. He appreciated their efforts, but was still very disappointed.

Friends learned Clay had taken a large loan backed by the value of Ashland. He had to pay campaign bills. He also wanted to help his son, Thomas, begin a business. Thomas's business soon failed and Clay was left with a large debt against his house. Friends quietly collected about fifty thousand dollars to help him. When Clay went to the bank, he was told his account was paid in full. He was speechless and teary after the cashier told him that his friends had covered the debt.

Manifest Destiny

The Texas Territory had been independent of Mexico for nine years, since 1836. Several European nations and Great Britain wanted it to remain that way. The territory's president, Sam Houston, had struggled all that time with too little money, too many problems, and almost no help.

Several months before the 1844 election, the House and Senate passed a joint resolution annexing the Republic of Texas to the Union. President Tyler delayed signing the document until March 1, 1845, three days before he left office. Tyler's action brought annexation to the nation's center stage. The next step was up to President Polk.

Polk firmly believed in "Manifest Destiny." The phrase first appeared in *The United States Magazine and Democratic Review* and John L. O'Sullivan of the *New York Morning News* popularized it.[10] It was the belief that America had a God-given right to govern the whole country from the Atlantic to the Pacific Ocean.

Oregon

Polk proceeded to challenge the British over the Oregon Territory. He wanted to end America's joint management of the region with Great Britain, which had begun in 1818. Despite the catchy campaign slogan, "Fifty-four Forty or Fight," Polk believed the northern border of the United States should not be at 54° 40' North latitude. (Latitudes are imaginary horizontal lines on the earth.) This included half of Canada. James K. Polk and Britain compromised after negotiating for a year and a half. They agreed to relocate the border to 49° North latitude. America's northern border finally was at the same latitude from the Pacific Ocean to the Great Lakes. Polk won what he had wanted all along. He signed the Oregon Treaty on June 15, 1846.

The United States began another war front a month before concluding the Oregon Treaty. Three issues were in dispute. First was the location of the southwestern border between Texas and Mexico. Second was the $2 million Mexico owed American immigrants. Third was Mexico's order to remove all Americans from its lands in Alta, or Upper, California, north to the Oregon border.

Mexico

Polk suspected Mexico of plotting with Britain to occupy Alta California. The British needed deep-water ports for the big sailing ships that traded with China. Polk ordered Secretary of the Navy George Bancroft to seize and occupy these ports if war began. Alta California's deep natural bays were in San Diego and San Francisco.

In April 1846, Polk ordered U.S. Army General Zachary Taylor, stationed with his troops at the Rio Nueces, to advance to the Rio Grande. Both countries claimed the disputed land between the two rivers. Polk ordered Taylor to consider any attempt by Mexico to enter Texas through the region as a hostile action.[11] Taylor found himself in such a

Zachary Taylor was commanding general of the American forces in the Mexican War, but he and Polk were not friendly. There was much jealousy among Taylor's officers. However, many remained loyal to him, and America won the war.

skirmish and Polk signed a declaration of war on May 13, 1846.

Clay thought of war as a tragic waste of human life. He worried about his son, Henry, Jr., who had joined the Second Kentucky Volunteer Regiment when the war began. Henry, Jr., was promoted to lieutenant colonel when he received orders to go to Mexico.

In late February 1847, Henry, Jr., was with Taylor's army near the town of Monterey, Mexico. Henry's regiment took part in a two-day battle where Mexicans outnumbered Americans four to one. The Americans won despite these odds.

Henry, Jr., was seriously wounded when a bullet hit his thigh. He ordered his men to leave with the pistols his father had given him when he left for the war. He asked the soldiers to "tell him I used them to the last."[12] After the men had gone, he lay quietly, waiting for the enemy. When the rebels

The Battle of Churubusco was one of the bloodiest of the Mexican War. It occurred near Mexico City on August 20, 1848, and lasted three hours.

discovered him, they stabbed him to death with their bayonets. A friend found him later and cut off a lock of hair to take to the Clays.

Henry and Lucretia were heartbroken to lose their beloved son in a war his father so greatly opposed. Clay first spoke publicly about the war the following November. He said, "This is no war of defense, but one of unnecessary and offensive aggression. It is Mexico that is defending her firesides, her castles and her altars."[13]

10

THE GREAT COMPROMISER

Henry Clay wanted to run for president again in 1848, but the Whigs chose General Zachary Taylor as their candidate. Clay had waited too long to announce his availability and everyone knew he had lost three previous presidential campaigns. Also, Taylor had grown popular due to his leadership during the Mexican War. Clay spent much of his time trying to improve his shaky health, but good results were temporary.

Troubled Senate

Clay was reelected to the Senate in 1848 after a six-year absence, during which he practiced law with his son, James, and traveled the country. Thousands came to see him and hear his speeches. On one occasion, when asked about his loyalties, Clay replied, "I have heard something said about allegiance to the South. I know no South, no North, no East, no West, to which I owe any allegiance."[1]

Congress faced a desperate problem. Many Americans realized they could no longer avoid confronting the issue of slavery. Many saw the system as a grave threat that could shatter the Union without warning.

Slavery issues surfaced again on December 3, 1849, when the California Territory petitioned to join the Union. Its constitution contained a "no slavery" clause. More than a year had passed since the Mexican War ended in 1848. America's government still could not decide how to handle slavery's expansion into areas that had been part of Mexico. If not settled soon, the problem could overwhelm the nation.

Looking for Compromise

Congress turned to the frail and ailing Senator Clay. He had rescued the nation from disunion twice before. The first time was the Missouri Compromise of 1820. Then came the Compromise Tariff of 1833, which removed South Carolina's threat to nullify the Tariff of 1832.

Clay had experience in dealing with tough situations. The Missouri Compromise had taught him the problems that go with trying to satisfy all sides about slavery. He considered his current mission the last chance to prevent civil war. He had to protect the existing equal balance between free and slave states.

On January 29, 1850, Clay practically begged his fellow congressmen to consider making compromises on this profoundly troubling question. Clay's long-time friend and opponent, Daniel Webster of Massachusetts, addressed the Senate for three hours on March 7. Although he opposed slavery on moral grounds, Webster said, "I speak today for the preservation of the Union."[2] He said that to attain this goal, the North must prepare to enforce the nation's fugitive slave laws. Not everyone agreed, but Webster had planted the idea.

On March 11, Senator William Seward of New York opposed Clay's ideas for compromise. He believed in a "higher law than the constitution" to resist slavery in the territories.[3] Seward supported the territory of California's admission to the Union "without conditions, without qualifications, and without compromise."[4]

Clay and the country lost a good friend when John C. Calhoun died on March 31. Too frail to speak, Calhoun had sat in the Senate to listen to his last speech be read by Senator James M. Mason of Virginia. In it, Calhoun expressed the fear that, "Disunion is the only alternative that is left us."[5]

Months passed as the Senate wrestled with grave problems. A Committee of Thirteen, composed of seven Whigs and six Democrats, finally produced an omnibus bill with four topics and one bill with a single topic. Clay presented the revisions to the Senate on May 8.

President Taylor opposed most of Clay's compromises because he wanted California to enter the Union as a Free State, without reference to slavery. Once, when Clay thought Taylor might veto a bill, he loudly announced, "Sir, I would rather be right than be President!"[6]

President Fillmore

Taylor contracted cholera on July 4, 1850, and died five days later. Vice-president Millard Fillmore assumed the presidency. Clay felt more confident with the omnibus bill in Fillmore's hands. He also suggested that Daniel Webster serve as Fillmore's secretary of state. Webster's influence would make all the legislation even more credible.

Clay pushed the omnibus bill in Congress again on July 22, when he gave credit to everyone for the compromise proposal. He appealed to his peers' "patriotic, nationalistic, moralistic sense" to help

America "remain a whole, undivided nation."[7] A friend of Clay's told Fillmore he had never heard Clay give a finer speech.

Action was being taken and Clay felt encouraged until the omnibus bill fell apart in late July. There were disputes over the location of the Texas boundary. His enemies were gleeful. Clay was tired and depressed. He went to Newport, Rhode Island, for his health, leaving turmoil and disorder behind him.

The Compromise of 1850

In Clay's absence, Democrat Senator Steven A. Douglas of Illinois, chairman of the Committee on Territories, reassembled Clay's omnibus bill into five separate bills. He followed what Clay had done with the Missouri Compromise of 1820. Douglas's efforts produced a new boundary that added 33,333 square miles to Texas.[8] When Clay returned, all the bills had been passed except one, which was approved on September 16.

The five bills that passed have since come to be called the Compromise of 1850. They called for the following provisions:

- Admit California to the Union as a Free State.
- Establish Texas's borders and give the territory $10 million to pay its debts. The new Texas would include the 33,333 additional acres it

gained due to Douglas's reworking of Clay's original omnibus bill.

- Require Texas to give up all claims to New Mexican Territory.

- Establish the New Mexico and Utah Territories.

- Allow residents of New Mexico and Utah to decide for themselves whether or not to make slavery legal. (This idea of allowing residents to choose for themselves was called "popular sovereignty.")

- Abolish the slave trade, but not slavery, in Washington, D.C.

- The Fugitive Slave Act: Require the federal government's active participation in returning slaves to their owners. Also, suspected fugitives did not have the right to a trial or to defend themselves during a trial or other judicial proceeding.

Douglas gave Clay full credit for this achievement. The compromise pleased most moderates. However, the United States had gone through enough trouble for Americans to know there probably would be more problems ahead.

Final Return to Ashland

Clay took the new train from Washington to Lexington. He had personal business to attend to and he wanted to review his finances. Well-wishers

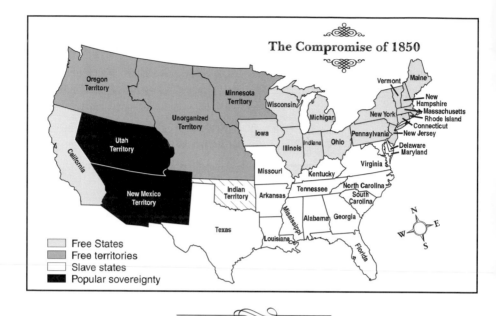

Henry Clay's Compromise of 1850 first introduced the idea of popular sovereignty.

greeted him everywhere. The Clays declined many of the invitations they received, preferring to be with their family.

Congress reconvened two weeks before Clay arrived in Washington. Freezing weather kept him indoors, and he slept poorly due to chronic colds and a deep, hacking cough. He was exhausted by mid-February and went home by way of a visit to Cuba.

He spent his time well in sunny Havana, Cuba, and stopped in New Orleans, Louisiana, before reaching Ashland on April 20, 1851. He spent months with his family, doing things he had missed when his children were young. He wrote his will and bought a plot in Lexington's new cemetery.

Last Days

Clay arrived in Washington on November 23 and went directly to the National Hotel. Congress greeted him with thunderous applause when he returned to his seat on December 1. The bitterly cold weather aggravated his cough and he sent for Dr. Francis Jackson of Philadelphia, who told him he had bronchitis. Clay realized his active days in the Senate were over and he resigned as of September 27, 1852. The date, nine months away, would allow the Whigs time to find the right candidate for his seat. It also kept the Democrats from nominating someone immediately.

As Clay's health declined, both parties kept him abreast of events and probed his still-agile mind for advice. Visitors noticed increasing signs of decline with each visit. His son, Thomas, came to care for him in April. He was at his father's bedside, their hands clasped tightly, when the Great Compromiser died of tuberculosis at 11:17 in the morning of June 29, 1852, at the age of seventy-five.

President Fillmore ordered the President's House draped in black. Thomas sent a telegram to the family in Lexington to inform them of Clay's death. Mourning bells rang throughout the city. All the stores closed. Washington became very quiet.

The next morning, July 1, military and civilian officials joined foreign dignitaries to follow Clay's funeral procession up Pennsylvania Avenue to the Senate. After a brief service, the casket was carried to the Rotunda of the Capitol to lie in state until 3:30 P.M. Clay was the first American to be so honored. President Fillmore, the Supreme Court justices, the Cabinet, senators, congressmen, foreign ministers, and many others came to honor him.

At the appointed hour, a crowd of dignitaries accompanied the casket to the train station for a week's journey to Lexington. The black-draped funeral car rolled slowly through the East, stopping at major cities in Maryland, Delaware, Pennsylvania, New York, and Ohio. Thousands lined the route in every state, waiting silently to pay their respects. Clay's casket was transferred to a riverboat and carried down the Mississippi to Louisville, Kentucky. His funeral procession arrived in Lexington at sunset.

Lucretia was too unwell to attend the funeral, but the line of mourners stretched back for over two miles. Following the Episcopal service, Henry Clay's flower-strewn coffin was placed in a vault until a special monument was ready to receive it.

11

REMEMBERING HENRY CLAY

Although Henry Clay's politics were often very controversial, he had friends everywhere. Clay made a positive impact on countless people, the famous and the unknown. According to author Thomas Rush, Clay was considered "the most charming of fellows, a huge hit with the ladies, he was the best of company, a manly man admired and liked by his colleagues, friendly and congenial, always ready to put aside political differences for a party, a card game . . ."[1]

Former congressman (and future president) Abraham Lincoln delivered a eulogy for his good friend in Springfield, Illinois, on July 6, 1852. Restating Clay's own comment, Lincoln quoted

Artist Charles Henry Niehaus made this statue of Henry Clay in 1929. It was a gift from the state of Kentucky to the National Statuary Hall Collection in Statuary Hall at the Capitol in Washington, D.C.

from a local journal saying, "He knew no North, no South, no East, no West, but only the Union, which held them all in its sacred circle . . ."[2]

Lincoln continued in his own words:

Throughout . . . he has constantly been the most loved, and most implicitly followed by friends, and the most dreaded by opponents, of all living American politicians. . . . in those great and fearful crises, the Missouri question—the Nullification question, and

The Famous Seven

In 1957, Senator John F. Kennedy of Massachusetts was chairman of a Senate committee to select the five most important senators in American history. Their portraits would hang on the wall of the Reception Room outside the Senate Chamber. The group quickly picked three men, but needed another two years to determine the other two. In 2000, the Senate selected two more members whose faces would join the five other senators on the Reception Room wall. The seven senators are now called the "Famous Seven."

The Great Triumvirate of the Nineteenth Century
- John C. Calhoun of South Carolina
- Henry Clay of Kentucky
- Daniel Webster of Massachusetts

Twentieth Century Senators
- Robert La Follette, Sr., of Wisconsin
- Robert Taft of Ohio
- Arthur H. Vandenburg of Michigan
- Robert F. Wagner of New York[3]

the late slavery question . . . endangering the stability of the Union, his has been the leading and most conspicuous part.[4]

On October 4, 1996, the Henry Clay Memorial Foundation in Lexington, Kentucky, honored U.S. Supreme Court Associate Justice Sandra Day O'Connor. In her remarks, O'Connor said, "Clay was an indispensable man. His career skipped across the entire surface of American political waters, and we still feel the ripples of his actions today."[5]

A number of Clay's ideas were ahead of their time. America in the mid-1800s began to evolve from a strictly agricultural society to one supported by manufacturing. New industries widened the range of available products. These were transported throughout the country on federally funded railroads and highways. Items made in America lessened the need for imported products. Today, the Federal Reserve System serves as the nation's bank to work with federal, state, and chartered banks. Clay had encouraged many of these ideas in his American system.

According to the noted American historian, Arthur Schlesinger:

> [Clay's] impact on American history was stronger than that of some of the people who beat him for the presidency, the office he most coveted [wanted to have] . . . and never won. If any president in that era could have prevented the Civil War, it would likely have been Henry Clay.[6]

Chronology

1777—Born near Hanover Courthouse, Virginia, April 12.

1781—Reverend John Clay dies; Henry is four years old.

1785—Attends Old Field School and St. Paul's Church
–1790   School.

1792—Becomes private secretary for George Wythe,
–1796   Chancellor of Virginia High Court of Chancery in
      Richmond.

1796—Studies with Attorney General Robert Brooke for
      one year.

1797—Is admitted to Virginia Bar Association; Moves to
      Kentucky.

1798—Acquires license to practice law in Kentucky.

1799—Marries Lucretia Hart in Lexington on April 11.

1803—Is elected to Kentucky Legislature.

1805—Is appointed Professor of Law at Transylvania
      University.

1806—Is sent to U.S. Senate to finish Senator John
      Adair's term.

1809—Serves as speaker of Kentucky Legislature; Is sent
      to U.S. Senate to finish Senator Thurlow
      Bruckston's term.

1810—Is elected to U.S. House of Representatives.

1811—Is elected speaker of the house on the first ballot
      on the first day of his first term in the House.

1812—United States declares war on Great Britain on
      June 1.

1814—Signs Treaty of Ghent in Belgium on December 24.

1815—Signs Trade Treaty with Britain on July 4; Is
      reelected speaker of the house on December 4.

1816—Supports charter for Second Bank of the United States; Presides at formation of American Colonization Society.

1819—Maine and Missouri request admission to the Union.

1820–1821—Negotiates and writes Missouri Compromise of 1820.

1821—Is first acknowledged as "The Great Compromiser."

1824—Introduces American System to Congress in March; All candidates in presidential race—including Clay, Adams, Jackson—do not get enough votes to be elected.

1825—With Clay's support, Adams is elected president by the House on February 9; Clay is appointed secretary of state; Adams and Clay are accused of a "corrupt bargain."

1828—Returns to Lexington.

1831—Runs as Democratic-Republican presidential candidate in December; Elected to United States Senate.

1832—Negotiates and writes Compromise Tariff Act.

1836—Is elected president of the American Colonization Society.

1839—Campaigns for Whig candidate William Henry Harrison.

1842—Resigns Senate seat and returns to Kentucky.

1844—Runs for president as a Whig, loses to Senator James K. Polk.

1849—Returns to the Senate in late fall.

1850—Negotiates and writes the Compromise of 1850.

1851—Resigns from Senate, effective in September 1852.

1852—Dies while in office in Washington, D.C., on June 29.

CHAPTER NOTES

Chapter 1. Henry Clay's Burden

1. Robert V. Remini, *Henry Clay, Statesman for the Union* (New York: W. W. Norton & Company, 1991), p. 724.

Chapter 2. The Early Years

1. Robert V. Remini, *Henry Clay, Statesman for the Union* (New York: W. W. Norton & Company, 1991), p. 3.

2. Ibid., p. 8.

3. Allen Johnson and Dumas Malone, Eds., *The Dictionary of American Biography* (New York: Charles Scribner's Sons, 1930), p. 174.

4. Ibid.

Chapter 3. Beginning a Political Career

1. David McCullough, *John Adams* (New York: Simon and Schuster, 2001), p. 505.

2. "Clay, Henry, 1777–1852," *Biographical Dictionary of the United States Congress*, n.d., <http://bioguide.congress.gov/scripts/biodisplay.pl?index=C000482> (January 23, 2003).

3. Paul M. Zall, *Jefferson on Jefferson* (Lexington: The University Press of Kentucky, 2002), p. 105.

4. Ibid., p. 106.

5. Richard Brookhiser, *America's First Dynasty* (New York: The Free Press, 2002), p. 71.

6. McCullough, p. 586.

7. Justice Sandra Day O'Connor, "Henry Clay & the Supreme Court," *Ashland: The Henry Clay Estate*, 2001, <http://www.henryclay.org/sc.htm> (January 23, 2003).

8. Maurice Baxter, *Henry Clay the Lawyer* (Lexington: University of Kentucky Press, 2000), p. 28.

9. Ibid., p. 29.

10. Ibid., p. 30.

11. Robert Remini, *Henry Clay, Statesman for the Union* (New York: W. W. Norton & Company, 1991), p. 46.

12. "Clay, Henry, 1777–1852."

13. O'Connor.

14. Ibid.

15. Ibid.

Chapter 4. Negotiations in Europe

1. William A. DeGregorio, *The Complete Book of US Presidents* (New York: Wings Books, 1997), p. 66.

2. Robert V. Remini, *Henry Clay, Statesman for the Union* (New York: W. W. Norton & Company, 1991), p. 108.

3. Ibid.

4. Richard Brookhiser, *America's First Dynasty* (New York: The Free Press, 2002), p. 78.

5. Ibid.

6. Ibid.

7. William Seale, *The President's House* (Washington, D.C.: The White House Historical Association, 1986), p. 134.

8. Brookhiser, p. 77.

9. Remini, p. 122.

10. Justice Sandra Day O'Connor, "Henry Clay & the Supreme Court," *Ashland: The Henry Clay Estate*, 2001, <http://www.henryclay.org/sc.htm> (January 23, 2003).

11. Paul M. Zall, *Jefferson on Jefferson* (Lexington: The University Press of Kentucky, 2002), p. 122.

12. Seale, p. 165.

13. Remini, p. 125.

Chapter 5. After the War

1. William A. DeGregorio, *The Complete Book of US Presidents* (New York: Barricade Books, Inc., 1993), p. 110.

2. Ibid.

3. Justice Sandra Day O'Connor, "Henry Clay & the Supreme Court," *Ashland: The Henry Clay Estate*, 2001, <http://www.henryclay.org/sc.htm> (January 23, 2003).

4. Robert V. Remini, *Henry Clay, Statesman for the Union* (New York: W. W. Norton & Company, 1991), p. 128.

5. Ibid., p. 130.

6. Ibid., p. 134.

7. Paul M. Zall, *Jefferson on Jefferson* (Lexington: The University Press of Kentucky, 2002), p. 121.

8. Catherine Allgor, *Parlor Politics* (Charlottesville: The University of Virginia Press, 2000), p. 98.

9. William Seale, *The President's House* (Washington, D.C.: The White House Historical Association, 1986), p. 128.

10. Allgor, p. 117.

11. Ibid., p. 116.

Chapter 6. Speaker of the House

1. William A. DeGregorio, *The Complete Book of US Presidents* (New York: Barricade Books, Inc., 1993), p. 109.

2. Robert V. Remini, *Henry Clay, Statesman for the Union* (New York: W. W. Norton & Company, 1991), p. 163.

3. DeGregorio, p. 82.

4. Ibid., p. 110.

5. "Annals of Congress, House of Representatives, 15th Congress, 2nd Session: History of Congress—Seminole War, p. 653," *A Century of Lawmaking for a New Nation: U.S. Congressional Documents and Debates, 1774–1875*, January 1819, <http://memory.loc.gov/cgi-bin/ampage?collId=llac& fileName=033/ llac033.db&recNum=324> (January 22, 2003).

6. Ibid.

7. Richard Brookhiser, *America's First Dynasty* (New York: Simon & Schuster, Inc., 2002), p. 86.

8. Justice Sandra Day O'Connor, "Henry Clay & the Supreme Court," *Ashland: The Henry Clay Estate*, 2001, <http://www.henryclay.org/sc.htm> (January 23, 2003).

9. Paul M. Zaul, *Jefferson on Jefferson* (Lexington: The University Press of Kentucky, 2002), p. 128.

Chapter 7. The Clays at Ashland

1. Robert V. Remini, *Henry Clay, Statesman for the Union* (New York: W. W. Norton & Company, 1991), p. 73.

2. William A. LaBach, *Henry Clay (1777–1852) and Lucretia Hart (1781–1864)*, June 30, 2002, <http:// members.tripod.com/~labach/hclay.htm> (January 23, 2003).

3. Remini, p. 200.

4. Ibid., p. 72.

5. Allen Johnson and Dumas Malone, Eds., *The Dictionary of American Biography* (New York: Charles Scribner's Sons, 1930), p. 177.

6. Remini, p. 214.

7. David McCullough, *John Adams* (New York: Simon & Schuster, 2001), p. 639.

8. Alan Cole Freeman, "Henry Clay (1777–1852)," *The i Freeman Genealogy Site*, 1998–2002, <http://homepages.rootsweb.com/~afreeman/hen_clay.htm> (January 23, 2003).

9. Remini, p. 282.

10. Ibid.

11. Ibid., p. 284.

Chapter 8. Washington Politics

1. Robert V. Remini, *Henry Clay, Statesman for the Union* (New York: W. W. Norton & Company, 1991), p. 293.

2. Ibid., p. 295.

3. Ibid.

4. William Seale, *The President's House* (Washington, D.C.: The White House Historical Association, 1986), p. 179.

5. Ibid.

6. Remini, p. 338.

7. Henry Clay, "#5391: John Bartlett, ed., *Familiar Quotations, Tenth Edition*," Bartleby.com, n.d., <http://www.bartleby.com/100/348.2.html> (January 23, 2003).

8. Remini, p. 329.

9. William A. DeGregorio, *The Complete Book of US Presidents* (New York: Barricade Books, Inc., 1993), p. 115.

10. "Henry Clay Dies," U.S. Senate, n.d., <http://www.senate.gov/artandhistory/history/minute/Henry_Clay_Dies.htm> (January 22, 2003).

11. Ibid.

12. Seale, p. 227.

Chapter 9. A Nation at War

1. William A. DeGregorio, *The Complete Book of US Presidents* (New York: Barricade Books, Inc., 1993), p. 144.

2. William Seale, *The President's House* (Washington, D.C.: The White House Historical Association, 1986), p. 229.

3. Ibid.

4. Thomas Rush, "Henry Clay (1777–1852): An Introduction," *From Revolution to Reconstruction . . . and What Happened Afterwards*, n.d., <http://odur.let.rug.nl/~usa/B/hclay/hclay.htm> (January 23, 2003).

5. Seale, p. 238.

6. Ibid., p. 239.

7. Ibid.

8. Allen Johnson and Dumas Malone, Eds., *The Dictionary of American Biography* (New York: Charles Scribner's Sons, 1930), p. 178.

9. Sam W. Haynes, *James K. Polk and the Expansionist Impulse* (New York: Longman, 1997), p. 54.

10. Ibid., p. 89.

11. John J. Farrell, *James K. Polk,1795–1849* (New York: Oceana Publications, Inc., 1970), p. 80.

12. Carol and Thomas Christensen, *The U.S.-Mexican War* (San Francisco: Bay Books, 1999), p. 160.

13. Ibid., p. 191.

Chapter 10. The Great Compromiser

1. Henry Clay, "#5392: John Bartlett, ed., *Familiar Quotations, Tenth Edition*," Bartleby.com, n.d., <http://www.bartleby.com/100/348.3.html> (January 23, 2003).

2. Robert V. Remini, *Henry Clay, Statesman for the Union* (New York: W. W. Norton & Company, 1991), p. 743.

3. Richard Brookhiser, *America's First Dynasty* (New York: Simon & Schuster, Inc., 2002), p. 127.

4. Remini, p. 743.

5. Ibid.

6. Henry Clay, "#5393: John Bartlett, ed., *Familiar Quotations, Tenth Edition*," Bartleby.com, n.d., <http://www.bartleby.com/100/348.4.html> (January 23, 2003).

7. Remini, p. 754.

8. Ibid., p. 758.

Chapter 11. Remembering Henry Clay

1. Thomas Rush, "Henry Clay (1777–1852): An Introduction," *From Revolution to Reconstruction . . . and What Happened Afterwards*, n.d., <http://odur.let.rug.nl/~usa/B/hclay/hclay.htm> (January 23, 2003).

2. Abraham Lincoln, "Abraham Lincoln's Eulogy on Henry Clay," *Speaker.gov: Documents*, n.d., <http://speaker.house.gov/library/texts/lincoln/clay.asp> (January 23, 2003).

3. "The 'Famous Five' Now the 'Famous Seven'," *U.S. Senate: Art and History*, n.d., <http://www.senate.gov/artandhistory/history/common/briefing/Famous_Five_Seven.htm> (January 21, 2003).

4. Lincoln.

5. Justice Sandra Day O'Connor, "Henry Clay & the Supreme Court," *Ashland: The Henry Clay Estate*, 2001, <http://www.henryclay.org/sc.htm> (January 23, 2003).

6. Arthur M. Schlesinger, *The Almanac of American History* (New York: Barnes and Noble, 1993), p. 223.

GLOSSARY

abolition—Act of ending or doing away with.

acquit—To be found innocent in a court of law.

alien—A foreign person who lives in another country, but is not a citizen.

amendment—A statement that changes an existing written document.

annexation—The incorporation of a territory or country into a nation

Cabinet—The main advisors to the president of the United States.

campaign—Military operation aimed toward a designated goal or objective; or duties undertaken in order to run for a political office.

caucus—A closed meeting of members of the same political party.

charter—A written document issued by an authority.

clause—Part of a document that is complete within itself.

effigy—A representation of a person, such as a large doll or painting.

force bill—Any bill introduced in Congress that authorizes the use of the military to enforce federal law.

indict—To bring charges against.

militia—Trained military group called to service as needed for a specific situation.

neutral—Not taking sides in a dispute or conflict.

omnibus bill—Any bill introduced in Congress that calls for or combines several unrelated laws.

sedition—Incitement of rebellion against the government.

tariff—A legislative bill that states the taxes due on goods imported from another country.

treaty—Formal, written agreement between two or more countries.

triumvirate—A group of three.

FURTHER READING

Burgan, Michael. *The Louisiana Purchase*. Minneapolis, Minn.: Compass Point Books, 2002.

Fish, Bruce. *The Speaker of the House of Representatives*. Broomall, Pa.: Chelsea House Publishers, 2001.

Ingram, Scott. *Aaron Burr & the Young Nation*. Farmington Hills, Mich.: Gale Group, 2002.

Lindop, Edmund. *James K. Polk, Abraham Lincoln, Theodore Roosevelt*. Brookfield, Conn.: Twenty-First Century Books, Inc., 1995.

Stone-Peterson, Helen. *Henry Clay: Leader in Congress*. Broomall, Pa.: Chelsea House Publishers, 1991.

Warrick, Karen Clemens. *The War of 1812: "We Have Met the Enemy & They Are Ours."* Berkeley Heights, N.J.: Enslow Publishers, Inc., 2002.

INTERNET ADDRESSES

Ashland: The Henry Clay Estate, Lexington, KY. ©2001 <http://www.henryclay.org/>.

Lincoln, Abraham. "Abraham Lincoln's Eulogy on Henry Clay." *Speaker.gov: Documents*. July 6, 1852. <http://www.speaker.gov/library/texts/lincoln/clay.asp>.

Rush, Thomas. "Henry Clay (1777–1852): An Introduction." *From Revolution to Reconstruction*. ©2001. <http://odur.let.rug.ni/~usa/B/hclay/hclay.htm>.

INDEX